THE FORD
FOUNDATION

D0143618

THE FORD FOUNDATION
The Men and the Millions

Dwight Macdonald

With a new introduction by

Francis X. Sutton

Transaction Publishers
New Brunswick (U.S.A.) and Oxford (U.K.)

10-17-90

HV 97 .F62 M25 1989
Macdonald, Dwight.
The Ford Foundation

New material this edition copyright (c) 1989 by Transaction
Publishers, New Brunswick, New Jersey 08903.
Originally published in 1955 by Reynal & Company, Inc.

All rights reserved under International and Pan-American
Copyright Conventions. No part of this book may be reproduced or
transmitted in any form or by any means, electronic or mechanical,
including photocopy, recording, or any information storage and
retrieval system, without prior permission in writing from the
publisher. All inquiries should be addressed to Transaction
Publishers, Rutgers--The State University, New Brunswick, New
Jersey 08903.

Library of Congress Catalog Number: 88-15400
ISBN: 0-88738-748-9
Printed in the United States of America

Library of Congress Cataloging-in-Publication Data

Macdonald, Dwight.
    The Ford Foundation: the men and the millions / Dwight
Macdonald; with a new introduction by Francis X. Sutton.
    p. cm.
    Reprint. Originally published: New York: Reynal, c1956.
    Bibliography: p.
    Includes index.
    ISBN 0-88738-748-9
    1. Ford Foundation--History. I. Title.
HV97.F62M25 1988
361.7'632'0973--dc19   88-15400

CONTENTS

INTRODUCTION TO THE
TRANSACTION EDITION

Dwight Macdonald's *The Ford Foundation: The Men and the Millions* remains after more than thirty years the only book-length account of the Ford Foundation that has been published.[1] Richard Magat's *The Ford Foundation at Work* (1979) describes how the Foundation has gone about its work, illustrating with case studies and summarizing the major programs to that date.[2] But Magat denied any aspiration to be Macdonald's continuator or supplanter. He and McGeorge Bundy, then retiring from the Foundation's presidency, called to scholars for a serious, full-length account of the Foundation. Special studies have since appeared, but their call for a big book carrying Macdonald's story on from 1956 remains yet unanswered.

One wonders why the Ford Foundation should be an uninviting or perhaps daunting subject. Institutional history is certainly not one of the more ingratiating literary genres, but even the big banks now seem to find willing chroniclers. Other foundations have found their historians or memoirs-writers, and there have been several lengthy accounts of the Ford family and the motor company, with Robert Lacey's *Ford: The Men and the Machine* and David Halberstam's *The Reckoning* current and lively.[3]

Perhaps the Ford Foundation has never again aroused as much public interest as it did in the years Macdonald recounts. The announcement in 1950 that it was ready to launch a new program with the riches that 90 percent of the Ford Motor Company's stock would bring caught the attention of the media all across the country. The sheer size of this new foundation was astounding. MacDonald wrote that in 1954 it spent four times as much as the Rockefeller

Foundation and ten times as much as Carnegie Corporation,[4] and its expenditures were very large in relation to the budgets of institutions that might look to it for help. Thus when Ford was committing $51 million in 1951, Father Ted Hesburgh became president of the University of Notre Dame with a budget of $9.7 million; or looking internationally at about the same time, the national University of the Philippines (which became a major Ford grantee) had an annual budget of about $3 million. The core budget of the United Nations Education, Scientific, and Cultural Organization (UNESCO) in those years was about $7.2 million.[5] With its riches still tied to the profitability of the Ford Motor Company it was not easy to say what the worth of the Foundation was, but it was clearly huge and growing. The year that Macdonald's book was published, the Foundation made its first sale of Ford Motor Company stock, realizing $641 million, and promptly gave away $548 million in an unprecedented largesse to American universities, liberal arts colleges, and hospitals. By 1960, the Foundation's capital of over $3 billion amounted to more than half the total endowment of all U.S. institutions of higher learning ($5.44 billion) and its annual budget was greater than the combined core budgets of the U.N. and its specialized agencies.[6]

The reactions of the American public to the appearance of this huge foundation were excitedly expectant. In the great anxieties over peace that this country felt (along with much of the rest of the world) at the time, there was particular attention to the promise that it might do something for preservation of the peace. Dwight Macdonald had no awe of foundations and had more modest expectations. He thought the Fifties were a silver age for foundations when they were reduced from old glories to "merely lubricating the gears of the status quo."[7] But Ford was so big that it might be a throwback and play the kind of role Rockefeller and Carnegie had played in the time of their greatness.

The Ford Foundation aroused lively interest in its early years not simply because it was so big. It was controversial in those years, in a way hardly ever repeated, even in the late Sixties when some of McGeorge Bundy's actions contributed to the political wrath that culminated in a 1969 tax act hostile to foundations. Ford's beginnings were in the time of McCarthyism. The journalists, Westbrook Pegler and Fulton Lewis, Jr., were tirelessly alerting their audiences to the dubious actions and purposes of the Foundation. There were two Congressional investigations of foundations, in 1952 and 1954, heavily colored by suspicions that they were leading the country toward socialism or otherwise undermining its character. These inquiries were a fine subject for Macdonald's talents and his chapter "The Inquisitors" is a concise and powerful depiction of American ambivalences toward foundations.

Another reason for the paucity of serious writing about the Ford Foundation may lie in its sheer weightiness of style and substance. Macdonald had a horror of the languages in which Ford has done its business. With his attentive eye and ear, he distinguished two strange languages at the Foundation- "philanthropese" for internal communication and "foundationese" for dealing with the world outside. He liked neither and wondered that men like Henry Ford II or the then President, Rowan Gaither, who could talk sensibly and even "perfectly rationally"[8] should adorn their public utterances about the Foundation with the vapid solemnities he derided. He found the famous Study Group report which set the Foundation's programs after 1950 to be written in a "contemporary dead language . . . a work of awesome earnestness, composed in the most stately foundationese, where meaning, such as it is, decently drapes itself in Latin rooted polysyllables."[9] The Annual Report he thought "a literary product that is somewhat more readable than the phone book and somewhat less so than the collected sermons of Henry Ward Beecher."[10] Macdonald was writing about the Ford Foundation and did not extend his gaze to the literary productions of other foundations, which would certainly not have fared much better under his scrutiny. Writing by foundations and about them has been much afflicted by solemnity and banality, like writing about foreign policy or economic conditions. Anxieties and urgencies assure tolerance for solemnity on these latter subjects but hardly on foundations. Respect for dignified institutions and notables is much less pronounced in our querulous present than it was when Macdonald was writing. But it has been hard to find an appropriate style for foundation history, and writing on them has continued to divide rather unfortunately into old-fashioned celebratory accounts and deliberately hostile, often quasi-Marxist, critiques. Macdonald's poised, ironic detachment has remained rare, and those tempted to devote their labors to foundation history have had few inspiring models.

The sheer abundance and diversity of what the Ford Foundation has done is also an evident deterrent to writing about it. Macdonald entitles one of his chapters, "What Hath Ford Wrought?" and he made an impressively accurate and manful attempt to answer his question. Macdonald was lucky to get to the Foundation early. Magat has said that his book is rather like a history of the U.S. that stops with the 1787 Constitutional Convention; This is a bit exaggerated; one might better say that it stops about the time of Thomas Jefferson. But even by 1955 there was a great array of activities to be surveyed and assessed. Unlike other journalists who have looked at a few examples and sought controversy or a thesis, Macdonald did not shirk the labors of a synoptic view, and he got the facts straight. One Ford staffer remembers reading a draft at the time and only being able to fault him on mixing up Merovingians and Carolingians in a learned allusion.

Dwight Macdonald brought unusual qualities to writing about the Ford Foundation. His name remains familiar to both older and younger generations as a member of the "New York intellectuals," whose literary and political exploits in the Thirties and Forties have been magnified by legend, and the subsequent rise of neo-conservatism. Mary McCarthy, Lionel Trilling, Sidney Hook, Philip Rahv, Hannah Arendt, and Delmore Schwartz were MacDonald's familiars, and he was the kind of man T.S. Eliot and Albert Camus wanted to see when they came to New York. He was a proper New Yorker, born there in 1906, going out of town for his education at Philips Exeter Academy and Yale but promptly returning in 1928 for a try in the "executive training squad" at Macy's, from which he was rescued after six months, when Henry Luce decided to start *Fortune*. Macdonald was seven years at *Fortune*, learning his trade as a journalist in the company of Archibald MacLeish, John Kenneth Galbraith, James Agee, and Louis Kronenberger. He quit in 1936 because he thought the editor had bowdlerized a series he'd written on the U.S. Steel Corporation which attacked its business efficiency and its treatment of labor. Learning at *Fortune* to master facts about big businesses and to tell them in a fashion that might hold a reader was a good start for a future author on the Ford Foundation.

There was a long odyssey to the Left between U.S. Steel and Ford that took him to *Partisan Review*, Trotskyism, anarchism, pacifism, and a heroic stint editing, writing, and proofreading his own little magazine, *Politics*. After funds and energies for *Politics* ran out he became a staff writer for the *New Yorker*, and it was as a series of articles for that magazine that his work on the Ford Foundation first appeared. Macdonald's intentions raised alarm at the Foundation. Its president, Rowan Gaither, wrote to a friend warning that Macdonald might "trap him into an interview,"[11] and Porter McKeever, who was Ford's public relations man at the time recalls that his first reaction to Macdonald's project was, "Is there any way to avoid it?"[12] But he had better second thoughts and tried to help Macdonald dig into what Ford had been and done. A thirty day project stretched into six months and the lengthy profile that became the 1956 book resulted. "Of course, when the book came out, there were screams all over the place," McKeever recalls, and he says that Gaither never forgave him for cooperating with Macdonald. But less touchy readers, inside and outside the Foundation, were entertained and instructed. The *Saturday Review* thought that "What U.S. scholarship needs, and is not getting by courtesy of foundation funds, is precisely the sort of clean, original, analytic work that Mr. Macdonald's book typifies."[13]

Dwight Macdonald had indeed succeeded in producing a book that stands out for its liveliness, independence, and fair-mindedness in the rather dreary terrain of writing on foundations. He could hardly have allowed himself to be dull. His opening sentence describing the Ford Foundation as "a large body of money completely surrounded by people who want some" has been endlessly quoted. It announced a tone that is sustained to the end without degenerating into flippancy and that carries the reader through a mass of accurately reported fact that a lesser guide would have made desiccating.

His book, in one of its merits, is a good account of the way some of the big foundations have worked. He did take too easily for granted that the Ford Foundation would follow in the models of Carnegie and Rockefeller, with strong professional staff and trustees of national prominence. Good journalist that he was,

Macdonald talked with Henry Ford II, Rowan Gaither, and enough others to get a firm sense of what went on during the first era when Paul Hoffman was president and Robert Hutchins his provocative lieutenant, describing the course of their downfall in 1953 and their replacement by Rowan Gaither and a new team of vice-presidents. A recent retracing of this history[14] does not basically fault Macdonald's account but takes it less for granted that Henry Ford II and the Ford family were as ready as they were to turn over power in the Foundation to others and to detach the Foundation from the Motor Company. Waldemar Nielsen's survey of new foundations established since Ford[15] is full of examples of founding families that quarreled among themselves and were unwilling to let go of power, either to "outside" trustees or staff. Ford's readiness to build up a sizable professional staff had models (which the study group had carefully reviewed) but again, subsequent examples show that it was not the inevitable course. The running of large foundations with minimal staff has subsequently become almost a vogue that was unforeseen in the years of Ford's beginnings.

Macdonald had a kind of sociological curiosity about the "philanthropoids" he found in the professional staff at Ford. He was not charmed, finding "something boring, unsatisfying, even irritating about the work of a great modern foundation like Ford."[16] But he was impressed with the eager friendliness and good will of these philanthropoids. They were unlike "the sedate elder statesmen of philanthropy who used to predominate in foundations a generation ago, gazing down patronizingly on aspiring grantees from their million-dollar ramparts."[17] He was sure that a cynic could not fully understand the Ford Foundation[18] and he dealt gently with the philanthropoids' difficulties in knowing what they were doing or ought to do.

It is perhaps curious that Macdonald was so mildly objective in his description of the bureaucratic hierarchy that he found at Ford. He had been through a period in his radical odyssey of struggle against "bureaucratic collectivism;" he had been a pacifist and in the years of editing *Politics* became a forerunner of the New Left in his insistence on the primacy of individual human beings, the virtues of small economic and political units, and non-violent resistance to government and other big organizations. In the 1950s when he was writing on Ford his political passions had quieted.

When they returned in force in the 1960s he must have observed with amusement Ford's efforts to make its bureaucracy more participatory and responsive to the times. But he was then too absorbed in the Vietnam war, draft resistance, poverty problems and the student movement to write again about Ford. His lasting political and social dispositions have been called anarchistic but they led him into no quixotic assault on Ford's organization; their influence showed more in his account of what Ford was doing.

Dwight Macdonald was too serious a man to confine himself to the internal history of the Ford Foundation. He reached out to set the Foundation in philanthropic history and to judge what it had done. He liked some of what he found (the overseas development programs,) regretted some things he did not find (arts and humanities programs) and was skeptical or critical about others (the Fund for Adult Education and the Fund for the Republic.) He kept trying to assess if the Ford Foundation would indeed be a throwback, using its unprecedented resources for great objectives as Carnegie and Rockefeller had done in earlier decades when government was less pervasive and foundation resources could matter more. He had read critics of foundations like Edouard Lindemann, Edwin Embree, and Abraham Flexner, who thought foundations stayed too close to safe, uncontroversial subjects and shirked the bold innovations they like to proclaim as their justification. His final assessment was pessimistic. He clearly thought that foundations ought to be ready to face controversy and to fulfill the pious hope of being on "the cutting edge of change." He saw the transition from Hoffman and Hutchins to Gaither as a retreat from the edge. He saw clearly that the Foundation had been scared by its critics ("Large foundations, like large corporations, are timid beasts")[19] and he treated the distribution of $548 million in 1956 to American colleges and hospitals as a public relations venture, successful as such but probably unnecessary. This great give-away was not an operation on the cutting edge of change but "in the very center of the status quo"[20] and certainly no throwback to the golden age.

A recent book about Dwight Macdonald's politics is entitled *A Critical American*.[21] He was certainly that but in the complex way that his radical politics and cultural conservatism combined to make him. For one so sophisticated from long immersion in the ideological currents of the times, the Ford Foundation was a subject not to be treated from a settled viewpoint. He had little or no sympathy with the conservative critics who dogged the Foundation in its first years, but he had done battle with enough liberals not to be excited by its liberal disposition. As a veteran of anti-Stalinist wars he dealt harshly with the Fund for the Republic that Hutchins directed as a "wholly disowned subsidiary" after he left the Foundation. Macdonald thought the Fund might have done better "if the Doctor and his staff were a little better instructed on Communism, say up to the high-school level."

The faith in Ford's Magna Carta, the Study Group Report, that solutions could be found to great world problems by collective efforts imbued with the spirit of scientific investigation, he viewed with unrelieved skepticism. He found Ford's style "scientific rather than cultural, utilitarian rather than aesthetic" and as such "more quintessentially American than the Carnegie and Rockefeller foundations."[22] He was among the first in a long line of critics who have wanted to see more support to individual creativity, which he thought to be the only real kind. He rather wistfully envisaged the possibility that Ford's millions might promote creativity in the arts and humanities, but he was writing a little too early to record the appearance (from 1957) of a major program to this end.

There was indeed still a strong leaning toward the scientific side at Ford in the late 1950s. Gaither wanted Ford to do more in support of the sciences and his successor, Henry T. Heald, who came to the Foundation in 1956 shortly after Macdonald's book appeared, was an engineer by training who set up a Science and Engineering program that lasted until McGeorge Bundy became president in 1966. But Heald eliminated the Behavioral Sciences Program, which the Study Group had recommended and Gaither had fostered. Macdonald, who cannot have had much sympathy with behavioral science, in label or substance, had the generosity of spirit to recognize the program as one of Ford's innovative efforts. Since its demise in 1957, Ford has had no broad programmatic interest in the behavioral sciences as such (though it has supported them abundantly in applications and in the pursuit of other objectives.)

Macdonald's vision of the Ford Foundation as "more scientific than cultural" was thus ambiguously realized in subsequent years.

The Arts and Humanities program had years of greatness in the 1960s, when its scale and innovative efforts made it a powerful influence on the American scene before it was overtaken by the National Endowments and the great rise in individual and corporate funding for the arts. It was popular with the trustees, as the behavioral sciences had never been.

And as the Sixties wore on and the values of the New Left spread through American society, an activistic spirit entered the Foundation that pulled it away from the study group's original vision of solving the world's problems through scientific knowledge. Particularly in the last chapter of the study group report, the peculiar vocation of foundations in the increase of useful scientific knowledge had been proclaimed. Ford has continued through the years fostering an enormous array of research institutions and programs, commissions and individual studies in the faith that this was the way to serve the "problem orientation" it had declared as guiding its work. Such a strategy puts trust in professional experts generating objective knowledge, and in organizations, typically governments, that can put such knowledge to use. In the overseas programs that Macdonald liked, Ford made great efforts to train social scientists and administrators and to build planning organizations and executive competences in the governments of developing nations. But this was not Macdonald's way. He was a "critical American," mistrustful of governments at home or anywhere, and of national policies, whether contrived by wise men or teams of experts.

Writing about Ford in the 1950s Macdonald could hardly have foreseen that the founding faiths of the Foundation would get shaken by values like his own, along with the rest of American society in the 1960s and 1970s. He would have been pleased to hear trustees denouncing "more studies for the shelf" and demanding action programs. In those years, Ford pulled away from governments and national policies toward engagements with local communities, voluntary associations, and with the basic needs of the poor and disadvantaged. Macdonald's depiction of Ford in the 1950s has the air of his resignation before the conservatism of the times and in his melancholy conclusion he foresaw more conservatism to come. For all his perspicacity, he did not feel how much Ford was then responding to the spirit of the times and would respond differently when that spirit changed, bringing it closer to his own critical values. For all their vaunted independence, foundations sway with the *Zeitgeist*.

Macdonald properly left open the answer to his questioning about Ford's potential. Would it act its size and mark the country or the world as Carnegie and Rockefeller had done? In the decade after Macdonald wrote it had great chances. In 1964 it reached its largest size with a capital that would amount to approximately $12 billion in 1987 dollars, and its size was still towering in relation to institutions and problems it sought to address. Some of the programs it then started have unquestionably left their marks. There were Merit Scholarships, the lift to ballet and theater in this country, the beginnings of the Green Revolution abroad, and the transformation of business schools and international studies in the universities at home. Serious assessment of these, and panoplies of other programs, need more attention from the historians, as do the bold initiatives of the Bundy era after 1966. If Macdonald were now to come back from the dead to assess them all he would have an exacting and rather confusing task. What, for example, would he make of the last in the list above-the great boost Ford gave to studies of China, Japan, the Soviet Union, Latin America, indeed all of the regions of the world? This was a program on which Ford spent about $350 million in the hope of equipping this country to act wisely and well in the new international power and responsibility it had after World War II. Have we indeed done better with China, the Soviet Union, Vietnam, Iran, Israel, or South Africa than we might have done without all this fresh scholarship and expertise? One could relish Macdonald's ironies! He would no doubt have taken delight in the way the program escaped its original conception and was captured by academics who had their own interests to deflect them from dutiful service of the national interest.[23] Deeper understanding of exotic places brings sympathies that have made many of our area specialists resolute critics not only of the U.S. government and its policies, but of the World Bank, multinational corporations, and indeed, principalities and powers generally. Humanistic area studies have flourished to a degree that might make Macdonald wonder if Ford continued to be "more scientific than culture," and a recent assessment of area studies centers faults them for neglect of foreign policy studies.[24] Money may have power but its hold diminishes sharply with time.

The decline in the relative size and power of foundations which Macdonald saw between the 1920s and the 1950s may have been temporarily arrested or reversed in the years around 1960. (The Rockefeller foundation also attained its greatest size in constant dollars in those years).[25] Ford's trustees then became so impressed with the rise in their assets that they worried about finding ways to spend more and more. Some of them scorned perpetuity and were ready, as indeed they were empowered by their charter, to dispose of the whole corpus in a few years. The rate of expenditure reached $367 million in fiscal 1966 and commitments were made in the years 1965-67 that exceeded income by some $463 million. If Ford was making a "big bang" it looked to be exploding itself to do so. When McGeorge Bundy came to the helm in 1966, he and the trustees decided that Ford ought be kept as a large foundation for the foreseeable future and annual expenditures were cut sharply, never again to rise to the exuberant levels of the mid-Sixties. The largest cuts were made in funds that had been flowing to American colleges and universities in the Heald years. Bundy was very good with figures, and he saw that the bounding growth of American higher education was diminishing the impact foundations could have on it. He pointed out in his report for 1966 that U.S. expenditures on higher education were growing at 14 percent per annum and Ford ambitions that seemed feasible in 1960 could no longer be sustained. A similar growth in international development expenditures was also making Ford less weighty overseas. By 1970, the regular budgets of the UN and its specialized agencies had grown to $400 million plus large voluntary contributions. And in the 1970s inflation and adverse capital markets brought worse times for Ford. Its assets shrank beneath $2 billion and by 1979 its annual expenditures (in current dollars) reached a low of $107.8 million. It was still the largest foundation but no longer a towering giant.

The excisions and adjustments made by the foundation in this great contraction from the middle of the Sixties to the end of the Seventies were of a sort that Macdonald might have approved. The overseas programs were reduced but the parts of them directed to basic needs in food production and population were protected, and heightened emphasis on equity and human rights appeared. At home, Bundy's sermon in his 1967 President's Report on the struggle for Negro equality as "the first of the nation's social problems" was heeded all through his presidency and by his successor, Franklin Thomas, after 1979. The disadvantaged in American society-Blacks, Hispanics, American Indians, and the poor in general-became the central domestic concern of the Foundation in education, housing, urban neighborhoods, civil rights, and political participation. In its style, the Foundation sought to be active in concrete problems and local settings. Policy studies inevitably persisted, but the main thrust of the National Affairs Program was toward community development corporations across the land rather than toward macro-economic issues, and the education program focused on opportunities for the disadvantaged, resisting complaints that the Foundation cared no more about the national pinnacles of excellence. In its staffing and governance, the Foundation sought the authenticity of representation from those it aimed to assist. The board had long talked of black membership and less firmly of women (Henry Ford II was resistant). The first non-American came on the board in 1966, the first black in 1968 and the first women in 1971 and 1972. The old days were past when Macdonald found the board an establishment of leading businessmen, university presidents, publishers, and a judge, all white, all male.

In many ways, the Ford Foundation thus came in the last years of Macdonald's life (he died in 1982) to much closer conformity with his ideas and values than it was when he wrote about it in the 1950s. It had constantly to reckon with governments, at home and overseas, but it followed the times in a more reserved and critical attitude toward their capacities and benevolence. Like Macdonald, it believed more in starting with real people where they were, and seeing to it that wherever possible, these people had voices of their own. Such motivations had never been absent-there was passionate concern about democracy in the first years, both at home and abroad; and India's community development program, which had major support from the Foundation in the 1950s, embraced nearly all the grass-roots, participatory principles of the 1970s. But it took the critical populist upsurge at the end of the 1960s to weaken faith that the Foundation's prime vocation lay in helping government, great universities, and research centers. We are perhaps still too close to these recent years to know the measures in which Ford's response was to the mood of the times, to the decline of its financial powers, or to the predilections of its leadership.

Ford remained too big, too prudent, and too anchored in the diversity of American society to follow Macdonald in his radicalism. It has never ceased to be "utilitarian rather than aesthetic" and it would have irritated Macdonald to know that it seriously considered abandoning the arts and humanities entirely in its travail of the 1970s. But broadly speaking, it moved toward ideas Macdonald proclaimed as a lonely voice in the 1940s, long before the great chorus that broke forth in the 1960s and still echoes with us.

Francis X. Sutton
September-October 1987

Notes

1.   William Greenleaf's *From These Beginnings: The Early Philanthropies of Henry and Edsel Ford*, 1911-1936. Detroit, Wayne University Press, 1964 is a kind of prehistory; Greenleaf went on to write "The Ford Foundation: the Formative Years," giving the history to 1956, but it was never published and rests in typescript in the Ford Foundation Archives.

2.   Magat's book is subtitled "Philanthropic Choices, Methods, and Styles," Plenum Press, New York and London, 1979.

3.   Neither book has much to say about the Ford Foundation.

4.   *The Ford Foundation* (hereafter The FF). p. 4.

5.   Figures for Notre Dame from a N.Y. Times story on the occasion of Father Hesburgh's retirement, June 13, I, p. 14 and Nov. 15, I p. 1, 1986; on the University of the Philippines from

a monograph by Harry Case and Robert Bunnell, *The University of the Philippines: External Assistance and Development*, Michigan State Universty, 1970, available as report #004175 in Ford Foundation Archives; on the United Nations, from Mahdi Elmandjra, *The United Nations System: An Analysis*, London, Faber and Faber, 1973, pp. 228-229.

6.   Figures from U.S. *Statistical Abstract* (1979) and Elmandjra, *loc. cit.* whose figures show total core budgets (not voluntary contributions) of $130.5 million when the Ford Foundation was expanding $163 million.

7.   The FF, p. 49.

8.   Ibid., pp. 138-39.

9.   Ibid., p. 101.

10.   Ibid., p. 103

11.   Rowan Gaither to William Webster, Nov. 29, 1954, in Gaither papers, Box 12, folder 145, FF archives.

12.   Porter McKeever, Oral History, FF Archives, p. 15, and conversation.

13.   Review by Fred Rodell, June 2, 1956, quoted in article on Macdonald in *Current Biography*, 1969, p. 279. Charles Poore in the N.Y. Times, May, 15, 1956, p. 29 thought "the most entertaining and informing study the Ford Foundation has brought into being so far is Mr. Macdonald's own book about it."

14.   Francis X. Sutton, "The Ford Foundation: The Early Years," *Daedalus*, Winter 1987, pp. 41-91.

15.   Waldemar A. Nielsen, *The Golden Donors: A New Anatomy of the Great Foundations* New York, Dutton, 1985, pp. xi+468.

16.   The FF, p. 124

17.   Ibid., p. 97.

18.   Ibid., p. 64.

19.   Ibid., p. 171.

20.   Ibid., p. 169

21.   Stephen J. Whitfield, *A Critical American: The Politics of Dwight Macdonald*, Hamden, Conn. Archon Books of Shoestring Press, 1984, pp. x+179.

22.   The FF, p. 93.

23.   Cf. Robert A. McCaughey, *Inrternational Studies and Academic Enterprise: A Chapter in the Enclosure of American Learning*, Columbia University Press, New York, 1984, pp. xviii+301.

24.   Richard D. Lambert et al. *Beyond Growth: The Next Stage in Language and Area Studies*, Association of American Universities, Washington, 1984, pp. 163ff.

25.   Rockefeller reached its peak in 1964, the same year as Ford. Figures courtesy of Mr. Jack R. Meyer, Treasurer, Rockefeller Foundation.

THE FORD FOUNDATION

CHAPTER 1

HOW MUCH AND WHO

THE FORD FOUNDATION, which in 1953 moved its headquarters to New York City from an estate in Pasadena that was known to the staff as Itching Palms, is a large body of money completely surrounded by people who want some. The Foundation is in the business of giving away cash, its function as defined in its charter being "to receive and administer funds for scientific, educational, and charitable purposes, all for the public welfare and for no other purposes." It is by far the biggest wholesaler in this peculiarly American field of private enterprise. Last year, its capital consisted of ninety per cent of the stock of the Ford Motor Company. On the Foundation's books, this was given the value, for tax purposes, of $417,000,000, but its real value, as measured by the earnings of Ford Motors, was at least $2,500,000,000. This is considerably more than half as much money as all the other foundations in the country have among them. The Ford Foundation's liquid capital, which corresponds in a general way to an individual's checking account, fluctuates between $60,000,000 and $100,000,000, depending on the time of year. (Only six other foundations are known to have *total* capital of over $100,000,-000.) The Foundation began to spend big money in 1950, when it gave away $24,000,000, and has continued on a rising scale ever since. Its 1954 spending came to just short of $68,000,000, which is four times what the second largest foundation, Rockefeller, normally spends in a year and ten times the annual spending of the third largest, the Carnegie Corporation. It is also as much as all American foundations together spent in any one year up to and including 1948, and it is about a quarter of the total spent by all American foundations last year.

All of the foregoing statistics, massive as they are, have proved to be but the prologue to the swelling theme of the magnitudinous immensity of the Ford Foundation. In the first place, the Foundation early in 1956 put on the market the first block of its Ford holdings, thus finally letting the public into what for decades had been by far the largest privately-owned business in the country. The sale, which was the biggest single offering of common stock in Wall Street's history, consisted of about one-fifth of the Foundation's Ford stock and brought in some $643,000,000. In the second place, last December the Foundation made an even more sensational announcement: it stated that in the next eighteen months it would give away $500,000,000, or most of what it would realize from selling its stock. This was not only by far the largest single benefaction in the history of American philanthropy, which operates in a large and dashing way but never on anything like this scale, but it also was $150,000,000 more than the Foundation itself had been able to give away in the whole twenty years of its existence up to then. The sum, which was a special, one-time appropriation outside the Foundation's regular program, is to be divided as follows: $210,000,000 to help raise faculty salaries in the country's private liberal-arts-and-sciences colleges and universities, all 615 of them; $200,000,000 to "improve and extend services" in the country's private, non-profit hospitals, all 3,500 of them; and

$90,000,000 to "strengthen instruction" in the country's privately-supported medical schools, all 42 of them.

Since bigness does not bore the American public, the Ford Foundation has been chronically in the headlines. It is becoming the kind of folklore symbol the Ford car once was—the first thing that pops into many people's minds when philanthropy is mentioned. There was the time that a California swindler, arrested for passing bad checks, told the cops that he had spent the money to buy uniforms for a boys' football team and expected to be reimbursed shortly by a grant from the Ford Foundation; there was the South American couple who drove from Paraguay to Detroit in a 1927 Ford, which they hoped to sell to the Foundation; and last summer the belligerent Patrick McGinnis, who was then still president of the New Haven railroad, told an audience of commuters, apropos of a new charge for parking in station lots, "If it costs me money, it's going to cost you money, because I'm a businessman, not the Ford Foundation."

Despite the growing tendency to regard the Foundation as a symbol, there is an almost incredible amount of confusion as to what the Foundation is and does. Westbrook Pegler is of the opinion that the Ford Foundation is a "front for dangerous Communists," while *Pravda* rather inclines to the view that "the real business of the Ford Foundation is the sending of spies, murderers, saboteurs, and wreckers to Eastern Europe." The Honorable B. Carroll Reece (Rep.), of Tennessee, has warned Congress that there is "important and extensive evidence concerning subversive and un-American propaganda activities of the Ford Foundation," while the Czechoslovakian Home Service Radio has broadcast, "So that future United States espionage agents will lack for nothing, the Ford Foundation has donated sums running into the millions."

The speculations of many Americans are less lurid but not much better informed. Indeed, although the Foundation's name is constantly coming up in the press and in talk, it would appear that a substantial number of them aren't sufficiently informed to speculate at all; at any rate, a recent Gallup Poll found that more than half of those interviewed had never even heard of the Ford Foundation, which would seem to indicate a rather cursory reading of the front pages. Gallup asked the forty per cent who said they *had* heard of it, "Just in your own words, what is the purpose of the Ford Foundation, what does it do?" About a third of the answers were wrong by the most liberal marking system: "Gives people work; it's a good factory," "All about better cars," "To help crippled children," "It is a peace pact that has gone to the Red side," "They want labor to do a day's work," "To study diseases and such," and so on. And most of those who had some slight inkling of the Foundation's actual nature—less than a third of the whole population—were on the vague side, giving answers such as "Helps education" and "Supports worthwhile research projects." It might, therefore, be interesting to see what, in fact, the Ford Foundation *has* been doing with All That Money.

The precise sum that the Ford Foundation gave away in 1954 was $67,777,741. The operation was performed by some two hundred and forty people—the trustees, a group of fourteen eminent citizens that includes Chairman Henry Ford II, who is also president of the Ford Motor Company; about forty staff members, headed by President H. Rowan Gaither, Jr., who have something to say about how the money is spent; thirty workers in field offices in Karachi, Beirut, Rangoon, Djakarta, and New Delhi; and around a hundred and sixty clerks, stenographers, and other employees who work at the Foundation's headquarters, which occupy eight floors of a gleaming new office building at Madison Avenue and Fifty-first Street. The money was handed out in a hundred and eighty-two grants, the largest of which was for $25,000,000, given to the Fund for the Advancement of Education, and the smallest for $900, given to Princeton so that Professor Kazuo Midutani, of Kobe University, could spend two more months in this country to complete a study of international trade. The biggest slice of the money—$34,000,000—went for education; $18,000,000 was spent on international programs; and the remainder was allotted to economics, public affairs, and the social, or, as the Foundation calls them, the behavioral sciences. The purposes for which the money was spent were extremely—in fact, excessively—varied, and included contributing to the development at New York University of a stove operated by sunlight ($45,000); building and financing for five years a Center for Advanced Study in the Behavioral Sciences, in Palo Alto, California ($3,-411,590); enabling the Committee on Disaster Studies of the National Research Council of the National Academy of Sciences to make a study of how people behave in floods, hurricanes, fires, explosions, and other depressing contingencies ($194,400); acquiring current Soviet publications for the Library of Congress ($16,925); training Haverford College students to work on the Gold Coast of Africa ($44,500); furnishing a research room in the New York Public Library in memory of the late Frederick Lewis Allen, of *Harper's*, who was a trustee of the Foundation when he died ($25,000); establishing training centers for village crafts in India ($407,575); building lecture halls and a library at the Free University of Berlin ($125,000); looking into the effects on readers of the recent merger of the Washington *Post* and *Times-Herald* ($12,991); making it possible for Yale scholars to examine the economic behavior of households ($60,000) and Stanford scholars to consider "the rejection of leadership opportunities in British politics" ($15,000); developing a program of international legal studies at the law schools of Harvard, Columbia, Stanford, California, and Michigan ($4,950,000); financing the publication in the *Atlantic Monthly* of supplements of translated Greek, Brazilian, Arab, and Indonesian writings ($150,000); helping the Detroit Board of Education perfect a new method of using audio-visual materials in teaching French ($7,038); aiding Dr. Albert Schweitzer's literary and philosophical studies ($10,000); and giving general support to the Brookings Institution ($1,000,000), the Council on Foreign Relations ($1,500,000), the Fund for Adult Education ($7,500,000), the Harvard Business School ($2,000,000), and a number of other weighty institutions, among them the Institute of Business Administration of the University of Istanbul ($385,000).

Rowan Gaither succeeded Paul Hoffman—Truman's Marshall Plan administrator, Eisenhower's adviser, and now chairman of the Studebaker-Packard Corporation —as president of the Foundation in 1953. He is of medium height, average build, and indeterminate coloring; his clothes are subdued, his neckties low-keyed, and he would be a hard man to pick out in a crowd; he has a roundish face and smallish features of the sort that don't look the same in any two photographs. His voice is low, with traces of both Southern drawl and Western twang; his manner is informal but reserved, friendly but discreet, institutional but not pompous; he is a shy glad-hander, a public-relations man with a highly developed sense of privacy. Unlike his predecessor, a man of expansive plans and pronouncements, which proved his undoing with the trustees, Gaither is almost wholly unknown to the public, having for years specialized in running research and philanthropic organizations in a reassuringly unobtrusive way. He has been called "a genius at putting together a functioning team," "a great little coöperator," "the perfect chairman," "a man with a mind like an I.B.M. machine," "the compleat administrator," "Henry's yes man," "the trustees' chosen instrument," and other things, but never "a personality." Asked which of the many activities of his Foundation appeal to him the most, he replies, with a pale smile, "I don't think it would be diplomatic to answer that. A judicial attitude is desirable in this department."

Keeping a cold, impartial watch over the intricate workings of the Foundation, Gaither mediates, without passion or prejudice, among the special interests of grantees, trustees, and the public. Half his working time is spent conferring with his staff, reading reports, and writing letters and memoranda. The other half goes into consulting with the trustees and with important and/or knowledgeable people who may or may not want a grant (at the moment, that is; practically everybody will, sooner or later). "It's part of my job to keep informed," he says. "So I try to be alert to opportunities of seeing people who don't want money." But even from veteran prospectors, with a dozen applications for grants up their sleeves, Gaither often manages to extract useful information. For he is an expert and patient listener, and three-fourths of being a foundation executive is listening without committing oneself.

The Gaithers are an old Maryland family, descended from Lord Baltimore's secretary; the town of Gaithersburg, in that state, is named after them. One branch drifted South, settling in Natchez, where, to give him the full name he never uses, Horace Rowan Gaither, Jr., was born in 1909. A year later, his maternal grandfather became governor of Oregon, and the family moved to Portland. Horace senior got a job in a bank there, and later became a bank examiner in San Francisco. In 1923, he and some friends, who put up the capital, founded the Pacific National Bank of San Francisco, of which he was the president until his death three years ago. Horace junior went to grammar school and high school in Piedmont, across the Bay from San Francisco, and then to the University of California. "We lived in modest circumstances," Gaither recalls. "Dad didn't make much as a bank examiner, and even after he had his own bank, it was a small one." All through school and college, Gaither had odd jobs—driving bakery trucks; doing farm work in the summers, at two dollars a day; pumping gas on weekends. At the University, where he was manager of the baseball team and president of his fraternity, he majored in history. He graduated in 1929. The following year, he entered the University of California Law School and married Charlotte Castle, who had been his girl since their sophomore year at Piedmont High and who is, so far as anyone knows, the only woman in his life.

Gaither graduated with honors from law school in 1933. It was the bottom of the depression, and he was glad to be offered, as an outstanding law graduate of that year, a $200-a-month job with the Farm Credit Administration, in Washington. He returned to California in 1936 to work in the San Francisco law firm of Cooley, Crowley & Supple, and became a partner the next year. In 1942, he took a job that proved to be the turning point of his career—that of assistant director of the Massachusetts Institute of Technology's Radiation Laboratory, in Cambridge, Massachusetts, a wartime organization that developed scientific devices, notably radar, for the armed forces. His job was to coördinate the work of the scientific staff and to act as liaison officer between the Laboratory and the armed services. Thus, at thirty-three, Gaither began to play the roles he has specialized in ever since—an organizer of research and a middleman between brains and capital. In Cambridge, he also came into close contact with scholarly and scientific groups for the first time and, in particular, made an important friend—the late Karl Compton, who was then president of M.I.T. After the war, Gaither went back to his law practice in San Francisco. In 1948, he was called in to help convert RAND (military code name for Research and Development) into the Rand Corporation, a private firm that now does research for the Air Force on everything from new kinds of explosives to the nature of the

Soviet Politburo. The conversion, of course, necessitated making Rand financially independent of the Air Force, and to this end Compton, who was a trustee of the Ford Foundation, introduced Gaither to Henry Ford II. He made such an impression on Ford that the Foundation not only gave Rand $1,000,000 for working capital but asked Gaither to organize and head a committee to prepare a report on how the Foundation, which up to then had been mostly a local Detroit affair, could best spend the huge income from the money it had just inherited from Edsel and Henry Ford.

The Study Report that Gaither and his committee came up with in 1949, after a year of research, became the Magna Carta of the new and greater Ford Foundation that began to flourish in 1951 under Hoffman. Gaither was made one of four associate directors of the Foundation, and devoted one or two days a week to Foundation business and the rest to his law practice and to Rand, of which he had been chairman since the 1948 change-over. When, early in 1953, he succeeded Hoffman as president, he resigned from his law firm, but he remained, and still is, chairman of Rand. He is also a director of Chromatic TV Laboratories, a California company that is developing a new television color tube invented by a friend of his— Ernest O. Lawrence, the Nobel Prize physicist. This enterprise got under way several years ago when Lawrence showed some rough sketches of his tube to Gaither, who organized the company and sold a half interest in it to Paramount Pictures for $1,000,000, which is now being used to get the tube into commercial production. Gaither expects it to become the standard tube for color television once it goes on the market, and he is a little embarrassed by the possible profits. He is helping Lawrence with the tube because he will go to a lot of trouble for a friend and because he feels that scientists are underpaid. "But how

Henry Ford II, son of Edsel, grandson of the first Henry, and president of Ford Motors, is chairman of the board. He was in the class of 1940 at Yale ("Ford will go into manufacturing," predicted the editors of the class-book, accurately enough), where he got his "Y" managing the crew, was on the business board of the *Record*, belonged to Zeta Psi, Book and Snake, the Amalfis, and the Haunt Club, was nicknamed "T," and failed to graduate. "They thought I was too stupid, I guess," he says, with a determined smile. (His brother Benson, who is also on the Foundation's board, went to Princeton, and didn't graduate, either.) Sober, solid, stoutish, a plain, downright sort of person, Henry II is not brilliant, but he has the modesty of common sense. When, in 1945, he became president of the Ford Motor Company, he did not himself try to reorganize and modernize the company, which was then losing some $10,000,000 a month, but instead called in three former executives of General Motors—Ernest R. Breech, L. D. Crusoe, and D. S. Harder. The team, headed by Mr. Breech, who recently became the company's first board chairman, has done a good job. In 1954, for the first time since 1935, Ford sold more cars than Chevrolet; last year Chevrolet recaptured the lead, but only by a slim margin.

Henry II, like the Rockefeller grandsons, is an heir to a great business fortune who seems to have developed that sense of responsibility and public obligation that also distinguishes some of the sons of the British upper classes. He says he enjoys being chairman of the Foundation—"It's very interesting"—and estimates that in 1954 he put in about a month on the job, including two days he spent taking part in a movie made to educate the company's executives and dealers about the Foundation. Asked recently what part of the Foundation's work has interested him especially, he replied, "I think people are generally interested in what they have some contact with personally.

I think I get the greatest kick out of the Free University of Berlin, because I was there and talked with Mayor Reuter and some of the others." Henry II gives the impression that while he feels it his duty to devote as much time to the Foundation as seems necessary, this is an interruption of his *real* job, which is running the company. "I rarely take a positive position on any program until the staff has acted on it," he says. "I never want to be an advocate. If I got mixed up in all that, I'd never get anything done around here." (The "here" refers to his not very plush office in the huge Ford Motor Company administration building, at Dearborn, Michigan, over whose portal is incised the incontrovertible maxim: "INDUSTRIOUS APPLICATION OF INVENTIVE GENIUS TO THE NATURAL RESOURCES OF THE EARTH IS THE GROUNDWORK OF PROSPEROUS CIVILIZATION.") He explains, "I don't see most of the mail that comes here addressed to me as chairman of the Foundation, unless it's from a personal friend. It's just passed along to Gaither. If a friend or a business acquaintance comes in or writes me about the Foundation, I pass him along, too." Catholics sometimes write Henry II about grants (he was converted, by Bishop Sheen, when he married Anne McDonnell, a Catholic girl), but he simply passes their letters along as well, without comment. He showed no concern over a 1954 grant of $600,000 to the Population Council, perhaps because, although the Council's remedies for overpopulation include birth control, the Foundation's staff tactfully limited the scope of the grant to the non-biological aspects of the subject.

On the other hand, Henry II takes action when he feels it is necessary. Three years ago, when he came to the conclusion that his friend and mentor Paul Hoffman was not doing a good job as president of the Foundation, he did not hesitate to persuade the trustees to replace him with Gaither. He is genuinely puzzled when critics of the Foundation accuse it of being Leftist. "The American Legion used to claim we were full of Communists," he says. "I never found any. If I had, I would have got them out quick. Once I was called a Communist myself, at a social gathering, by a very influential woman. I didn't bother to answer. What's the use? It's too easy. You call someone a Communist when you don't agree with him. I don't agree with McCarthy, so I suppose that makes me a Communist." Not agreeing with McCarthy is not the only way Henry II deviates from the views of many of his fellow-industrialists. Possibly influenced by Hoffman, he is something of a globalist. He is for the reduction or abolition of tariffs on foreign goods, including automobiles; he favors more American aid to backward countries; and two years ago he was a conscientious member of the American delegation to the General Assembly of the United Nations.

In addition to President Gaither, the trustees of the Foundation at present consist of one judge (Charles E. Wyzanski, Jr., of the United States District Court, in Boston); two newspaper publishers (John Cowles, of the Minneapolis *Star* and *Tribune*, and Mark F. Ethridge, of the Louisville *Courier-Journal*); three educators (Donald K. David, formerly dean of the Harvard Business School; Laurence M. Gould, president of Carleton College, in Northfield, Minnesota; and Julius A. Stratton, provost of the Massachusetts Institute of Technology); and seven businessmen (the two Ford brothers; Frank W. Abrams, former chairman of Standard Oil of New Jersey; James B. Black, chairman of Pacific Gas & Electric; James F. Brownlee, a partner in the private banking firm of J. H. Whitney & Co.; John J. McCloy, formerly High Commissioner for Germany and now chairman of the Chase Manhattan Bank; and Charles E. Wilson, formerly president of General Electric and now chairman of W. R. Grace & Co.).

The trustees get $5,000 a year, which is unusual; the trustees of most foundations serve without pay. The Ford trustees, however, are exceptionally busy at their job, since the Foundation is still young enough to have to work out all sorts of matters that have become routine in older foundations. Thus, the finance committee—Brownlee, Mc-Cloy, Gaither, and Wilson—met nineteen times in 1954, mostly to consider the delicate and complex problem of when and how to sell some of the Foundation's Ford stock to the public. Like their chairman, the Ford trustees estimate that they spend about one month a year on the Foundation's business; they meet for two days four times a year, put in another two days on homework prior to each meeting, and devote about two weeks, here and there, to informal conferences and phone talks with President Gaither and his staff and to special subcommittees and assignments. McCloy, for example, says he attended seventy-two Foundation sessions in 1954, including the nineteen meetings of the finance committee. He also spent some time reinvesting the Foundation's liquid assets in whatever part of the short-term money market was yielding the best return at the moment, and since the Foundation generally has from $60,000,000 to $100,000,000 in that kind of loose change lying around, this is something of an operation. Judge Wyzanski, for another example, went on a six-week European tour for the Foundation in 1953, interviewing some fifty people about its affairs and writing a fifteen-page report for his fellow-trustees.

Since Gaither became president, in 1953, the trustees have taken a more active part in running things than they were able to do under the rambunctious Hoffman. In fact, some critics feel that the balance of power has swung rather too far away from the staff. "*Our* trustees are well disciplined," an executive of one of the older foundations said not long ago, with a side glance at Ford. "They know it is bad form for a trustee to try to get money for his own pet causes or to encourage end runs around the staff. A thoroughly trained trustee won't even let a friend use his name in approaching his foundation. Our trustees are there to decide general policy—specific grants are up to us, not them. This business can only be run efficiently on the basis of the trustees' having full confidence in the staff." Such a strict division of labor is still far off at Ford, where trustees have been known to promote their pet causes, give friends introductions to the staff, and otherwise behave in an undisciplined manner.

CHAPTER 2

THE INQUISITORS

LARGE FOUNDATIONS are practically unknown on
the Continent, where the rich are in the habit of holding
on tight to what they have and the State discourages private foundations by denying them tax exemption and regu-
lating them strictly. (In the spring of 1955, the European
Cultural Foundation was formed in Geneva, with an initial
capital of $125,000, which it will try to increase to $10,-
000,000; it has been described by the *Times* as "the only
private international foundation in Europe comparable in
conception though not yet in financial strength to the
great American private foundations.") There are a few
fairly large foundations—such as the Nuffield Trust—in
England, where there is a tradition of private philanthropy. But it is only in the United States that wealth has
been amassed on a large enough scale to make its disposal
a problem. Some American millionaires have found other
solutions—in yachts and fancy living, like Diamond Jim
Brady and Bet-a-Million Gates; in art-collecting, like Frick
and Morgan; or in just keeping the stuff, like Hetty Green,
Russell Sage, and other classic misers—but by and large
they have been sensitive to the fact that in this country
the accumulation of vast fortunes is not considered, as it is

in older and more cynical societies with generally accepted class distinctions, the private affair of the accumulator. The democratic tradition puts pressure on the rich to "do good" with their wealth; even Russell Sage's tightly grasped millions finally ended up, through his widow, as the foundation of a foundation. Of the thirteen major family-interest groups which President Roosevelt's Temporary National Economic Committee in 1940 identified in the ownership of the 200 largest non-financial corporations, all but one had their own foundations. The exception was the Pitcairn family. The other twelve were: Ford, Rockefeller, DuPont, Mellon, McCormick, Hartford, Harkness, Duke, Pew, Clark, Reynolds, and Kress.

It is all most bewildering to Europeans. "The French seem totally unable to understand the Ford Foundation," a youthful American sociologist recently wrote home from Paris, where he was working on a Ford-financed project. "The 'inside-dopesters' are sure of the explanation of such an otherwise incredible institution—to 'cheat' the government out of tax money. This appears to be the residue of some unfortunate American's effort to explain the relationship of our tax system to the rise of the private foundation. But there is simply no comprehension of foundations as social institutions. Few French intellectuals are even aware that there *is* a Ford or a Rockefeller Foundation, much less that setting up a foundation has become a routine procedure for Americans with money. Some suspect that these foundations are some sort of quasi-official intelligence agencies working for the State Department under cover of scientific respectability. Giving one's private goods for public welfare on such a scale just doesn't fit into French experience. Of course, the motivation *is* complex, and Americans don't wholly understand it, either. But they believe it. The French just don't believe it."

One of the things that French intellectuals wouldn't believe if someone told them is that the Ford Foundation is not merely a devious way of advancing the economic interests of Ford Motors. They would presumably be baffled by the fact that in 1949, when the Foundation came into the bulk of the estates of Edsel and Henry Ford and consequently shot up from a good-sized institution to a gigantic one, its trustees decided to expand the range of their spending to global proportions, instead of using the extra money to buy good will at home, where it would be more likely to help the sale of Ford cars. Nor would they have understood Henry Ford II when he recently told a reporter, "I very rarely talk about the Foundation with people in Detroit. Nobody brings up the subject much. Malcolm Bingay, who used to write the editorials in the Detroit *Free Press*—he's dead now—used to attack the Foundation all the time because he thought we ought to spend all our money in Detroit, or at least in Michigan. But if we had, it wouldn't have done nearly as much good."

The French intellectuals would be further confused by the fact that the big foundations, in general, and Ford, in particular, have, in recent years, been harassed by two special Congressional investigations and regularly denounced by journalists of the extreme Right. These attacks have come to center more and more on the Ford Foundation, whose monthly intake of "drop-dead" mail rose last fall from a dozen or so letters to several hundred. The usual horrendous edifice of charges, including un-Americanism, subversion, eggheadism, and general Left deviationism, has been supported—or, rather, propped up— by the usual mixture of midget quarter-truths, mammoth innuendoes, and cosmic implications. This must be perplexing to the shades of Andrew Carnegie and John D. Rockefeller, not because of the attacks, for they, too, got plenty of unfriendly attention, but because in their day the winds of criticism blew from precisely the opposite quarter. Then the foundations were being charged with conspiring to promote reaction, and the charges were brought not only by liberals but by solid citizens like George W. Wickersham, of the eminent Wall Street law firm of Cadwalader, Wickersham & Taft. Shortly before the First World War, when the Rockefellers were unsuccessfully trying to get a federal charter for their projected foundation, Mr. Wickersham, who was Taft's Attorney General at the time, wrote to his boss that it was a sinister scheme for perpetuating vast wealth and "might be in the highest degree corrupt in its influence." And two years later, when Carnegie gave $75,000,000 in bonds of the United States Steel Corporation to his newborn foundation and suggested that some of the income be used for pensions of $25,000 a year to former Presidents of the United States and their widows, there was such a public uproar about "currying Presidential favor" that the foundation hastily dropped the idea. In those days of trustbusting, muckraking, and general suspicion of "malefactors of great wealth," gift horses were likely to lose all their teeth when they were looked in the mouth. (Later, Carnegie did venture to leave, in his will, pensions to Taft and to the widows of Cleveland and Theodore Roosevelt.)

In 1915, a Commission on Industrial Relations, headed by Frank P. Walsh, a Kansas City lawyer who later became chairman of the New York State Power Authority, devoted a lot of attention, almost all of it unfriendly, to foundations. A special target was the Rockefeller Foundation, which, after being refused a federal charter, had finally managed to get itself incorporated in New York State. The Foundation had been inept enough to commission W. L. Mackenzie King, a young sociologist who later became premier of Canada, to make a study of labor relations shortly after the Ludlow Massacre, in which militiamen shot up and burned out a tent colony of strikers against the Rockefeller-controlled Colorado Fuel & Iron Co. Asked by the Walsh Commission about this coincidence, John D. Rockefeller, Jr., replied, with more candor than discretion, "Our office staff is a sort of family affair. We talk over all kinds of matters of a common interest. We have not drawn sharp lines between business and philanthropic interests." One of the Commission's reports recommended that foundations be limited in size and spending, and that they be regulated by the government; a minority of the members even suggested that Congress dissolve the Rockefeller Foundation and distribute its capital among the unemployed, on the theory that it represented profits that should rightfully have been paid out in wages. Although Congress took no action, the Rockefeller trustees were alarmed. They decided to confine the Foundation's activities thereafter to the politically safe fields of physical science and medicine, except for such innocuous grants as the $100,000 they appropriated to the Y.W.C.A. in 1917 "for the protection of girls in the neighborhood of military camps," and another $100,000 they contributed to the war fund of the Knights of Columbus that same year. (The latter gift was made a few months after the Knights had attacked the Foundation as "a menace to democracy," and the trustees were probably relieved to have it accepted— at about the same time Mayor Hylan indignantly turned down an offer from the Foundation to build New York City a new hospital for drug addicts, complaining that the money was "tainted.")

At the Walsh hearings, a few sympathetic, though cautious, voices were raised on behalf of foundations. Dr. George Kirchwey, former Dean of the Columbia Law School and father of Freda Kirchwey, of the *Nation*, while admitting that great private wealth was in itself disturbing, went so far as to say that the situation was "distinctly bettered by the transfer of that wealth from an individual to a corporation, which is legally, to a certain degree at least, responsible to the public," adding, "I should not think that the possession of great wealth . . . by the Rockefeller Foundation . . . would be as apt to cause irritation and discontent and unrest as the possession and conspicuous use of that same wealth by Mr. Rockefeller himself." And Samuel Untermyer, though no friend of big business, testified, "I do not share the fear and distrust of these foundations. . . . They are doing incalculable public good and no harm. Happily, their conduct does not to any appreciable extent reflect the devious methods by which those fortunes were accumulated, nor the views or policies of their founders on economic questions."

Mr. Untermyer's estimate was a just one. The great foundations have stuck mostly to "non-controversial" fields, such as medicine, education, charity, and the physical sciences, and when they have gone into more dangerous areas, as some of them began to do in the twenties, after the Walsh Commission scare had died down, they have by no means necessarily reflected their founders' views. The Russell Sage Foundation, founded by the widow of the most notorious skinflint of his day, almost singlehandedly created the profession of "social work," with all its elaborate Freudian trappings. The Guggenheim Fellowships have certainly not been awarded on a basis of artistic conservatism. Nor did the Rockefellers at all impede the march of progress when they allowed Beardsley Ruml to spend $14,000,000 of Laura Spelman Rockefeller Memorial funds between 1922 and 1929 in order to put the social sciences on the academic map. In short, the great foundations have proved more responsive to the values of the professionals who run them and of the academic community on whose borders they operate than to those of the rich men who founded them. This, of course, is just what alarms the most articulate viewers-with-alarm of our day—those of the extreme Right. Where a Samuel Untermyer was happy to see little connection between the foundations' policies and those of their founders, a Westbrook Pegler boils over regularly when he thinks how Henry Ford's money is being used to thwart Henry Ford's social and economic philosophy, which was almost as narrow as that of Mr. Pegler himself.

In the case of the Ford Foundation, the viewing with alarm was initiated by the Chicago *Tribune* with a news story it printed in 1951, under the headline "LEFTIST SLANT BEGINS TO SHOW IN FORD TRUST"—the slant being the participation in various Ford Foundation activities of such people as Paul Hoffman, who, as head of the Marshall Plan, had "given away ten billion dollars to foreign countries"; Dr. Reinhold Niebuhr, professor of Applied Christianity at the Union Theological Seminary ("pinko tie-ups"); Supreme Court Justice Owen J. Roberts, "a world government advocate"; and Frank Altschul, "a Roosevelt Republican and retired international banker." The Hearst columnists have been sounding the tocsin diligently ever since. "Many books and various studies have been financed by tax-free grants from some of these foundations," Fulton Lewis, Jr., wrote several years ago. "In effect, the American people are paying more taxes to finance so-called scholars who work diligently to beat out our brains and change our traditional way of life into something more Socialistic." And George Sokolsky observed, "Henry Ford . . . made nearly all his money in this country, but Paul Hoffman, who is spending that money, seems to prefer to pour it into remote bottomless pits and to expend it for meaningless purposes, such as an investigation as to why the world is full of refugees, when, as a matter of fact, it always has been." Mr. Sokolsky also put forth a positive suggestion: "Why cannot some of the money the Ford Foundation is piddling away on trivia be used constructively for the saving of opera?"

Even the Foundation's ponderously respectable trustees look fishy to Westbrook Pegler. After defining Hoffman as "a hoax without rival in the history of mankind," he cast a cold eye on the eight trustees who were in office at the time. While grudgingly conceding that four of them (including two Fords and the Dean of the Harvard Business School) "seem sound enough," he felt that "the best that can be said of the political wisdom of the others [who included a former chairman of Standard Oil of New Jersey and a former president of General Electric] is that they are flighty." Although sure the Foundation is up to something dubious, Peg has never been able to make out just what it is. This worries him. "We will have to start watching these outfits in this strange new development in our affairs lest they use the power of enormous tax-free pools of money to destroy the liberties of the American people," he wrote in February, 1952. "They are in reckless hands. . . . That is the way queer international things get going." Six months later, his column bore the hopeful headline "FORD FOUNDATION IS FRONT FOR DANGEROUS COMMUNISTS," but the only relevant information underneath it was that Associate Director Milton Katz was "a Frankfurter man of the same group that insinuated dangerous Communists into our Government," and that there was some kind of connection, doubtless pernicious, between the Foundation, Eisenhower, Henry (China Boy) Luce, and "the Marshall Plan squanderbund." "I find it beyond my ability at the moment to establish the master plan of these strange associations and activities," Peg confessed. "I will continue, however, to offer you verified facts and my best efforts at interpretation." Progress has been disappointing. "STRANGE EVENTS, ASSOCIATIONS PROVE PUZZLING" another Pegler column was headed, and a third began, "There is a very important and sinister political mystery concealed in the mixed activities of the Ford Foundation under Paul Hoffman and Robert Hutchins, the *Time-Life* propaganda empire of Henry Luce, and the political works of William Benton, the Social-Democratic Senator from Connecticut." At the end of the column, the mystery remained as mysterious as ever.

Efforts have been made to strike at the Foundation through the Ford Motor Company. The Constitutional Educational League, whose headquarters, on Madison Avenue, are near those of the Foundation, though considerably more modest, will, for five cents, send anybody a pamphlet practically all of whose contents are included in its title: *Ford Motor Company and American Bar Association Help Communist Conspiracy by Joining Plot Against "McCarthyism."* The pamphlet is advertised by a leaflet written in more sprightly terms: "DO YOU OWN A FORD, MERCURY OR LINCOLN? If you do . . . then you are unwittingly giving support to the Communist cause thru Ford Company profits being spent by the leftist-leaning Ford Foundation." According to Henry Ford II, the campaign has had no discernible effect on sales, which in the last few years have climbed to an all-time high. "The dealers send us in letters from customers accusing the Foundation of being Communist and warning us they'll never buy another Ford," he says. "But I don't bother much with that sort of mail. Why should I?"

The Congressional investigations of the foundations, however, are another matter. There have been two since 1952, which is par for the course even today. Both were instituted on the ostensible ground that the republic was or might possibly be or maybe had been or perhaps was going to be in danger from the foundations. In reality, both were merely episodes in Republican factional politics. (It would be hard to say which fact about Alger Hiss some of the Republican committee members were more delighted to spread on the record—that Dean Acheson wouldn't turn his back on him, or that Dulles and Eisenhower, as trustees of the Carnegie Endowment for International Peace, were loyal supporters of Hiss in his

$20,000-a-year job as president of that foundation.) Since the big foundations are now closer to the academic than to the business community, they were *a priori* suspect among Right Wing Republicans, who were not reassured, either, by their large overseas spending or by their dabbling in the social sciences. Furthermore, the Fords and Rockefellers took boxes at the 1952 Republican Convention and were conspicuous among those who won the nomination for the Eisenhower internationalists against the Taft isolationists, while Paul Hoffman, then head of the Ford Foundation, was not only the former head of "the Marshall Plan squanderbund" but also one of Eisenhower's chief political advisers. It was clear that the remedy for these evils was a Congressional inquiry—in fact, two—into the effect of foundations on the American way of life.

In the first investigation—by a House committee under the chairmanship of the late Eugene Cox (Dem.), of Georgia—the strategy misfired, because the Democratic leaders, who were still in control of the House, boxed in the impeccably Americanistic chairman with less dedicated colleagues. In consequence, the Cox Committee chose competent men with an objective approach as its counsel and its research director, and conducted the hearings fairly. As they proceeded, even Chairman Cox was moved to admit that he had experienced "some change of heart." The Committee's report, issued in January, 1953, was brief and judicious. It stated that "on balance, the record of the foundations is good" in the matter of Communist infiltration, the chief exceptions being their support of the Institute of Pacific Relations during its rufous period and the employment of Alger Hiss as president of the Carnegie Endowment for International Peace. The report considered "the question of whether the foundations have used their resources to weaken, undermine, or discredit the American system of free enterprise . . . while at the same time extolling the virtues of the Socialist state" and concluded that "the testimony does not establish this to be the case," adding helpfully, "Many of our citizens confuse the term 'social,' as applied to the discipline of the social sciences, with the term 'Socialism.' " The members were unruffled even by the fact that foundations spend money abroad: "The Committee believes that these international activities are motivated chiefly by consideration of the welfare of the American people and as such are entirely praiseworthy."

One member of the Committee, however, the Honorable Brazilla Carroll Reece, a former Chairman of the Republican National Committee, while signing the report, appended an ominous postscript proposing "a more comprehensive study," because "the Committee has had insufficient time for the magnitude of its task." This was puzzling, since the Committee not only had held twenty-eight hearings (of which Mr. Reece had been able to attend only three) but had also sent out to the larger foundations a questionnaire that ran to twelve pages of small type. ("There were a couple of months there when you couldn't get any top foundation people on the phone," a college official recalls. "They were all too busy answering the Cox questionnaire.") The explanation of Reece's calling for a new investigation was that he had been one of Taft's campaign managers, and so was especially disappointed by the Cox Committee's failure to "get" the Fords' and the Rockefellers' foundations.

Accordingly, in the summer of 1953 Reece arose in the House and asked for a repeat performance. "There is evidence to show there is a diabolical conspiracy back of all this," he declared. "Its aim is the furtherance of Socialism in the United States." Selecting the Ford Foundation as his principal target, he said, "Here is the last of the great American industrial fortunes, amassed in a competitive free market place in the last fifty years, being used to undermine and subvert our institutions. . . . The Ford Foundation—which is the wealthiest and most influential of all foundations—was not actually investigated by the Cox Committee." (The testimony before that committee of the Foundation's top executives covered a hundred and thirteen pages, and the Foundation's reply to the questionnaire seventy-five pages.) Reece's bill of particulars against the Ford Foundation was lengthy, ingenious, and absurd. It included charges that one of its executives had "served on a committee to welcome the Red Dean of Canterbury" during a visit to this country (the executive had signed a petition asking the State Department to let the Dean enter the United States, arguing that to keep him out would give the Communists a good talking point); that it had made a grant to "a person who wants to abolish the United States" (this ambitious character turned out to be Dr. Mortimer J. Adler, an advocate of world government); that another of its grants had tended "to promote Socialism" by enabling the Advertising Council to put out a booklet called *The Miracle of America* (the Council is a big-business outfit, and the book was praised by *Business Week, Banking*, and the Chicago *Tribune*, and was distributed by such Socialistic organizations as Republic Steel, General Motors, and Standard Oil of California); and that it was spending millions in "pro-Communist India" (the Associated Press reported from New Delhi around the time Reece was making his speech that the Indian Communist Party was demonstrating against the Ford Foundation's community-development program there). In building up this last point, Reece quoted from a speech that Cox had made two years earlier while proposing *his* investigation: "Over a period of thirty-two years, $45,000,000 of Rockefeller money was expended in China, most of it going to Chinese institutions of higher education. . . . Our boys are now suffering and dying in Korea, in part because Rockefeller money encouraged trends in the Chinese colleges and schools which swung China's intelligentsia to Communism." Reece's gloss on this was: "What has happened once can happen again, and I am sure that my colleagues in this chamber share my anxiety as to the future of India and what the Ford Foundation is doing there." The reasoning seems to be that since the Westernization of Asia gave an opening to the Communists, the West should now abandon Asia to them.

The state of the Congressional mind in 1953, when McCarthy and McCarran were riding high, was such that any proposal to "investigate Communism" was almost certain of a majority if it could ever be brought to a vote. The question that bothered Reece was how to get his bill out of the Rules Committee. It happened that he was a member of this committee and that the Eisenhower Republicans on it needed his help in getting an excess-profits bill onto the floor of Congress. An arrangement was reached: Reece agreed to back their bill, whereat they voted to release *his* bill, which the House passed at once, by a vote of two hundred and nine to a hundred and sixty-three. The results of this bit of statecraft, which set up another committee to investigate foundations, with Reece as chairman, were even more fantastic than might have been expected. The hearings, held during May, June, and July of 1954, were devoted largely to the animadversions of obscure crackpots and the scarcely more lucid testimony of the Reece Committee's staff. The long list of "charges" against the Ford Foundation in Reece's 1953 speech demanding the investigation was conveniently forgotten—nobody from the Foundation was even called on to testify—and attention was centered on all sorts of general complaints, including one to the effect that the foundations have overemphasized the inductive, or empirical, method that has been dominant in Western thought roughly since Descartes, at the expense of the deductive approach of Aquinas and other medieval philosophers, who argued from general principles to data, rather than the other way around. The Reece savants made "empiricism" a dirty word—or tried to. (In his 1953 speech, Reece had given a fine example of the deductive approach when he asked why the Ford Foundation hadn't financed "studies regarding the excellence of the American Constitution, the importance of the Declaration of Independence, and the profundity of the philosophy of the Founding Fathers.") Only one important representative of any foundation testified—Pendleton Herring, president of the Social Science Research Council, who was unkind enough to observe that the only country where deductive reasoning was still dominant was the Soviet Union. Several weeks after Herring's testimony, Chairman Reece announced that the hearings were over. He gave as his reason the obstreperous and obstructionist tactics of one of the Democratic members—Wayne L. Hays, of Ohio. "During one three-hour session," Reece complained, "Mr. Hays interrupted one witness two hundred and forty-six times"—or an average of considerably more than once a minute. Mr. Hays' tactics were indeed almost as demagogic as those of Mr. Reece, but two wrongs, etc. In any case, the significant fact is that the hearings were cut short before the foundations had their day in court.

In December, 1954, the Committee issued a majority report signed by its three Republican members and a brief dissenting report signed by its two Democrats. The majority report was a lengthy exercise—four hundred and sixteen pages—in irrelevance, insinuation, and long-range deduction. Over a third of it was a Who's Who of American intellectuals who had been "cited by the Attorney General of the United States or by various governmental agencies for associations and affiliations of a questionable character" and had been connected in one way or another with some foundation activity (*Perspectives USA*, a cultural magazine subsidized by the Ford Foundation, yielded a big crop). The report gave the full dossiers on all these goats—whom it separated from the sheep by printing their names in a special type each time they were mentioned throughout the rest of the report—some of them running to page after page of jumbled, unevaluated newspaper clippings and other snippets. Mere concern with Soviet Russia, whether pro or con, was apparently "questionable" in the eyes of the Committee, whose list included George F. Kennan because, first, a book of his had been reviewed in two Communist papers (whether favorably or otherwise is not stated); second, he "spoke on Communist China" early in May, 1950 (ditto); and, third, he "attacked witch-hunting of Communists" three weeks later.

In general, the majority report was a patchwork of data botched together to support two major propositions—that the social and cultural changes that have taken place since the McKinley administration are the result of a conspiracy by the staff employees of foundations, and that these changes are subverting the American way of life. ("In attempting to portray the historic changes of the twentieth century as the result of a conspiracy," observed President Gaither in the statement he filed with the Committee on behalf of the Foundation, "the theory ignores such factors as two world wars; an economic depression of global proportions; the emergence of the United States and Russia as world leaders of conflicting ideologies; the rise of nationalism and new nations in less developed parts of the world; and vast scientific and technical change.") On the latter score, after admitting reluctantly that it had come across little evidence that the foundations have supported pro-Communist activities, the report stated, "However, some of the larger foundations have directly supported 'subversion' in the true meaning of that term—namely, the process of undermining some of our vitally protective concepts and principles. They have actively supported attacks upon our social and governmental system and financed the promotion of Socialism and collective ideas." As "subversion" means undermining "protective"—or G.O.P.—principles, so "Socialism" means the economic policies of Roosevelt and Truman. "In the United States," Chairman Reece has observed, "Fabian Socialism has taken the name 'New Deal' and 'Fair Deal.'" If you can't lick 'em, redefine 'em.

This extraordinary document was a majority report in form only. One of the three Republican signers, Representative Angier Goodwin, of Massachusetts, added a note below his signature: "In signing this report, I do so with strong reservations and dissent from many of its findings and conclusions and with the understanding that I may file a supplementary statement to follow." Representative Goodwin did file a supplementary statement: "I dissent from the view that the foundations have rendered this country a great disservice by promoting Socialistic doctrine through . . . the social sciences; that the foundations are fostering Socialistic teaching in the schools to the detriment of true Americanism, and that . . . the foundations promote internationalism to the detriment of American interests. . . . Nothing has transpired in the proceedings of the present Committee to cause me to alter or modify the views I expressed in the Cox Committee report." In short, he disagreed with the main points of the Reece report and agreed with the diametrically opposite conclusions of the Cox Committee, of which he had also been a member; therefore—he signed the Reece report. This curious footnote to history went almost wholly unreported in the press, and Chairman Reece did not think it necessary to print either his colleague's note or his statement in the published record of the hearings.

The effect of the Reece report on the country at large was peculiar. Not only did most of the nation's newspapers, overwhelmingly Republican though they are, attack it—there were ten hostile editorials to every favorable one—but Dr. Gallup's investigators found that the Reece hearings and the report they led up to had, if anything, increased the popularity of the Ford Foundation. Early in 1954, before the hearings started, the public was asked: "In general, do you have a favorable or unfavorable opinion of the Ford Foundation?" Sixty-three per cent of those interviewed had never heard of the Foundation, thirteen per cent were indifferent to it, twenty-three per cent looked on it with favor, and one per cent were hostile. A year later, after the Reece report was out, the same question was asked again. This time, sixty per cent had never heard of the Foundation, eleven per cent had no opinion, twenty-seven per cent were favorable, and two per cent were hostile. Although it might be argued, and doubtless was by Reece's resourceful staff, that the negative vote had doubled while the positive had increased only fractionally, it was possibly more significant that the Foundation had picked up four votes to every one gained by Reece. The poll also showed that Republicans are better educated than Democrats, or at least read the papers more: Forty-six per cent of the Republicans queried after the appearance of the Reece report had heard of the Foundation, as against thirty-five per cent of the Democrats. There was, interestingly enough, almost no difference in the way Republicans and Democrats lined up pro or con on the Foundation, which suggests that the Reece and other recent attacks are expressions not of the Republican Party as a whole but only of a fringe of extremists.

CHAPTER 3

THE NATURAL HISTORY OF FOUNDATIONS

THE FORD FOUNDATION is a philanthropic institution, of which there are estimated to be roughly 499,999 others in this country today. These include all churches, most universities and hospitals, and a great variety of miscellaneous agencies through which private wealth is voluntarily turned over to public service. F. Emerson Andrews, of the Russell Sage Foundation, who is probably the leading authority on philanthropic giving, puts their total wealth at $40,000,000,000, and estimates that in 1954 they received about $5,401,000,000 as gifts, for disbursement in one way or another. These are big figures—much bigger than anything known in the same field abroad—but the conclusion that Americans are therefore a uniquely generous people must be tempered by the fact that $5,000,-000,000 is about what they spend each year on smokes and is $3,000,000 less than what they spend on liquor. Perhaps the only safe generalization is that this is a very big and a very rich country.

A foundation, like a corporation, is a fictitious person who is legally immortal. Plato founded his Academy before this concept had been developed, and hence could perpetuate it after his death only by willing it to someone —specifically, his nephew—who, in turn, had to leave it to someone else, and so on; although the method was cumbersome, the Academy lasted for 876 years, from 347 B.C. to 529 A.D., when the Emperor Justinian dissolved it on charges of unChristian activities. The Romans were the first to develop the legal concept of a corporation as an "artificial" person, and under the five "good emperors" (Nerva, Trajan, Hadrian, Antoninus Pius, and Marcus Aurelius), philanthropic foundations were encouraged throughout the Empire. The churches and monasteries of the Middle Ages were, in legal form, foundations; the great English ecclesiastical foundations, at the time Henry VIII expropriated them, owned from a third to a half of the wealth of the whole country. The private, non-religious charitable foundation has long been recognized in English law, and many precedents for foundations today go back to the Tudor period, especially the reign of Elizabeth. By the eighteenth century, endowing a foundation— or setting up a trust, which can be much the same thing —had become common practice among philanthropically inclined men of wealth. But the multi-million-dollar, general-purpose foundation for "the public welfare" or "the benefit of humanity" is a product of the American twentieth century. And the Ford Foundation is—quantitatively, at least—the climax of this evolution.

Most of the five thousand or so foundations in this country are of the traditional kind—rather small, and with much more modest concerns than the benefit of humanity. Fewer than five hundred of them have endowments of as much as $1,000,000, and only a dozen or so have over $50,000,000. They range in size from the Wilmington Foundation, which when last heard from had total assets of $849.61 and an annual budget of $1.51, to Ford, which is about two million times as big. They all have in common a happy exemption from taxes, under Section 501 (c) (3)

of the Internal Revenue Code, and a corresponding obligation to spend their money for non-profit-making purposes.
The range of these purposes, and of the motives for creating foundations at all, is almost as great as the range in their
size. That vanity often is a motive may be inferred from
the fact that five out of six foundations bear the name of
their founder. "Carnegie" has come to mean not steel but
libraries, "Guggenheim" not copper but fellowships, and
"Rockefeller" not oil but medical research, and the day
may come when "Ford" will mean not automobiles but
education. Another motivating force has been the feeling
that money is evil per se and must be apologized for by
consecrating it to philanthropy. Edmund Burke described
a foundation as "the useful fruit of a late penitence," the
Victorians spoke of it as "atonement," the muckrakers of
the early nineteen-hundreds wondered whether "tainted
money" could ever be purified, and the modern idiom
speaks of "guilt feelings." A Quaker heiress once established a foundation to help the educational work of Booker
T. Washington among Southern Negroes. "Thee does not
need to thank me," she wrote him. "It is I who needs to
thank thee—and I didn't do it to save my soul from Hell,
either!" The lady did protest too much.

To come down, or up, to the level of consciousness,
foundations have been created to further every conceivable
purpose, and some inconceivable ones. The Audiology
Foundation exists "to focus public attention upon the
handicap of deafness"; the Gravity Research Foundation
investigates the force of gravity, "with special reference
to its extended uses in connection with health, mental
activity, and power," and offers prizes to "persons who
discover a satisfactory screen, reflector, or absorber for
gravity that will reduce weight" (its trustees include Roger
W. Babson, who predicted the 1929 stock-market collapse,
and Clarence Birdseye, who gave us frozen foods); the
aim of the Robert Schalkenbach Foundation is "to keep

before the public the ideas of Henry George," and through subsidized lectures, classes, and reprints of the Master's works, it has preserved in being to this day a small but determined body of single-taxers; the Albert and Mary Lasker Foundation chiefly supports medical research but it also rewards services to the cause of birth control, or, in the constructive phrase its advocates prefer, planned parenthood; the Borah Fund for the Outlawry of War boils down to annual "peace conferences" on college campuses; the Bernarr Macfadden Foundation's object is "to propagate the principles of health building by natural means"; the Hat Research Foundation, which is not entirely unconnected with the hat-manufacturing industry, tries to discourage the recent tendency of men not to wear hats. There is, or was a few years ago, one foundation which has a near-monopoly on the raw material of foundations and which puts out a house organ called *Foundation Facts*. This is the Edward K. Warren Foundation, of Three Oaks, Michigan, which operates a recreation park. Mr. Warren's foundation is the chief owner of his factory, which turns out almost all the national production of featherbones, which, as everybody knows, are used in corsets to make the stiffening that makes a foundation a foundation.

A foundation may also serve as a remarkably uninhibited form of posthumous self-expression. The classic examples are English. A Victorian lady named Green established one to provide green waistcoats for other ladies named Green. An eighteenth-century misogynist named Thomas Nash left fifty pounds a year to the town of Bath "for the use, benefit, and enjoyment of the set of ringers belonging to the Abbey Church, Bath, on condition of their ringing on the whole peal of bells, with clappers muffled, various solemn and doleful changes . . . on the 14th of May in every year, being the anniversary of my wedding-day; and also on every anniversary of the day of my decease, to ring a grand bob major and merry mirthful peals, unmuffled . . . in joyful commemoration of my happy release from domestic tyranny and wretchedness." Americans are in the running, however. One man left money to pay a band to march around his grave once a year, another to pay for the illumination of his wife's tombstone. The Chappel Kennel Foundation, now extinct, had as one aim "a study of the problem of keeping dogs in city apartments." In 1930, Samuel Davis, of Mashpee, Massachusetts, left a fund to reward local schoolboys for "good, kind manners"; in 1938, the trustees asked the courts to let them spend the money some other way, because we "can't find enough mannerly boys to reward."

This country has even produced a spite foundation. In 1890, John Armstrong Chaloner, a descendant of John Jacob Astor, established a foundation to help Americans study art abroad. In 1897, he was committed to a New York lunatic asylum; three years later he escaped and fled to Philadelphia, where alienists pronounced him sane. After brooding about the matter for twelve years, he amended the charter of his foundation to include three new purposes: To crusade against antiquated lunacy laws, to publish satirical poetry—by himself—in the Shakespearean-sonnet form, and to keep his fortune from ever benefiting his brothers, who, he believed, had railroaded him into the asylum so they could get it. It was Chaloner, by the way, who, upon learning that one of his brothers, the painter and wit known as Sheriff Bob Chanler—the proper form of the family name was also involved in the feud—was about to marry the beautiful but tempestuous diva, Lina Cavalieri, sent him the famous "Who's loony now?" telegram. The question, it turned out, was an eminently sane one.

Two contemporary foundations, both of them among the twenty-five biggest, have a distinctly personal flavor—the Le Tourneau Foundation and the Longwood Foundation. The former owns almost all the stock of the R. G. Le Tourneau Company, the leading manufacturer of earth-moving machinery, and its founder and president, Mr. Le Tourneau, calls it "the Lord's Treasury," because its funds go mostly to "maintain camps for religious retreats in which its president often takes active part." The latter foundation recently inherited $50,000,000 from the late Pierre S. du Pont, the income from which it will try to spend on maintaining Longwood Gardens, on his estate near Philadelphia, "for public inspection, enjoyment, and education."

Some decidedly practical aims are also involved. It could hardly be expected that Americans would not see, and ex-ploit, the rich possibilities for combining business and phil-anthropic pleasure that a foundation offers. A simple ex-ample is that of a Wisconsin man who established a foundation that used its entire income to pay the salary of its research director, his wife. More complex specimens include some that are restricted to spending their money in areas in which the founder's customers live, such as the Frank E. Gannett Newspaper Foundation, whose opera-tions are limited to those towns that have Gannett news-papers. One state, Texas, exempts from taxes only such foundation spending as is kept within its boundaries, though this is probably less a matter of economics than of simple disbelief in the reality of the extra-Texan world.

In recent years, under the stimulus of higher business taxes, foundations have been put to strange new uses. They have been set up to accumulate tax-free capital for ambitious but impecunious Napoleons of industry. They have been employed to cut the cost of building or renting business property by means of an ingenious arrangement known as a "leaseback," whereby the property is sold to a founda-tion and at once leased back to the seller—who may even have lent the money for the purchase—at a rental that can be attractively low, since the property now pays no taxes.

The most direct way to escape taxes—until the Revenue Act of 1950 stopped it—was to reorganize a business as a foundation; the profits had to go to the foundation, but since they were tax-free, this did no harm either to the company's competitive position or to the salaries of its executives. These perversions of the foundation idea have had such results as the transfer of the ownership of the Mueller spaghetti company to New York University; the purchase from Macy's of its new San Francisco store for $4,500,000 by a foundation created by Yale University and given the improbable name of Connecticut Boola, Inc., which then leased the store back to Macy's for thirty-one years at $240,000 a year, to the mutual enrichment of Yale and the Strauses; and the creation of a New England textile empire, which culminated in control of the huge American Woolen Company's being taken over last year by the ambitious and Napoleonic Mr. Royal Little, of Textron, Inc. ("One of Mr. Little's trusts," Kenneth Fiester wrote in the *Nation* of April 9, 1949, "grew from $500 to $4,500,000 in eleven years, during which time it paid out only $50,000 to the supposed beneficiary and more than $200,000 to its trustees, including a United States Senator.") The worst of these abuses, though by no means all of them, were outlawed with the passage of the 1950 law.

The Ford Foundation itself is a product of the tax laws. If Edsel and Henry Ford had left their Ford stock to Edsel's children instead of to the Ford Foundation, the heirs would have had to sell most of the shares they had inherited in order to pay the inheritance tax. By giving the Foundation ninety per cent of the stock—all non-voting —the elder Fords avoided that danger, at least for a decade; the recent sale of a part of the Foundation's Ford holdings is a recognition that utopia can't last forever. "Without the very simple Ford Foundation—created by a document running only three double-spaced typewritten pages—the Fords would clearly have lost their control of the company," Berrien C. Eaton, Jr., observed in the *Virginia Law Quarterly* of December, 1949. In this respect, the Ford Foundation differs from the two other great general-purpose foundations—Rockefeller and Carnegie— which may be presumed not to have been founded to escape income or death taxes, since at the time of their founding neither of these taxes existed. And in this respect it resembles most of the foundations set up after the personal income tax became law, in 1913.

The motives for setting up a foundation are one thing, however, and the way in which it behaves after it has been set up is another. In its actual practices, the Ford Foundation resembles its two big pre-tax brethren, as do almost all the larger foundations born in recent years. Business considerations may have been the motive for starting these foundations, but the public welfare—or at least their trustees' notion of it—determines how they spend their money. A notable exception is the fourth biggest foundation—the $135,000,000 Duke Endowment. Founded in the twenties by the late James Buchanan (Buck) Duke, a tobacco-and-power magnate of the old, uninhibited school, the Duke Endowment is extremely private-spirited. Its indenture, which Buck Duke and his lawyers are said to have spent ten years perfecting, made Trinity College, in Durham, North Carolina, the principal beneficiary on condition that it change its name to Duke University, which it immediately did. It also "recommended" Duke Power securities "as the prime investment" of the Endowment, and it went on to stipulate that the trustees must see to it that the Duke Power system is properly managed, and must also act as trustees for the Doris Duke Trust, set up for the benefit of Doris and other Duke heirs; that the Endowment may sell none of its Duke Power holdings without the unanimous consent of the trustees; that the income must be doled out, after Duke University has received its share, in strictly apportioned percentages, to hospitals and col-

leges, "superannuated preachers, their widows or orphans,"
and rural Methodist churches and seminaries; and that all
the recipients must be situated in areas of North and South
Carolina served by Duke Power. Thus the interests of
Duke's heirs, his power company, his customers, his foundation, and God (Methodist Church, South) are all cun-
ningly knotted together. "What I mean is I've got 'em
fixed so they won't bother it after I'm gone," said Buck just
before he died.

Things have gone pretty far since Benjamin Franklin established the first important American endowment, in
1790. His purpose was simplicity itself compared to the
turgid intricacies the modern foundation gets itself into
in its efforts to spend its millions "all for the public welfare
and for no other purposes," as the Ford Foundation's
charter puts it. Franklin left a thousand pounds each to
the cities of Boston and Philadelphia, where he had grown
up and flourished, and specified that the money was to be
lent out, at interest, to married apprentices of upright behavior. "I wish to be useful even after my Death, if possible," Poor Richard wrote, in character to the last. Yet
even this relatively simple aim came into conflict with the
changeability of life; by 1860 there were no apprentices
left, upright or otherwise, and the bulk of the funds, which
had been piling up at compound interest, as stipulated by
the prudent donor, ultimately had to be used for more
modern purposes. The same sort of difficulty was encoun-
tered by most of the other early endowments, among them
the Magdalen Society of Philadelphia, established in 1800
to help "unhappy females who have been seduced from
the paths of virtue and who are desirous of returning to a
life of rectitude," which, although it was never in danger
of running out of clients, found it increasingly hard to
locate females willing to admit their fallen estate, and
finally, in 1918, changed its name to the White-Williams

Foundation and its field to "family problems"; Girard College, a Philadelphia school for orphans, founded in 1848 with an endowment of $2,000,000 (left by Stephen Girard) that has grown to $90,000,000, the problem now being where to find enough orphans; and the Bryan Mullanphy Emigrant and Travelers Relief Fund, established in 1851 "to furnish relief to all poor emigrants and travelers coming to St. Louis on their way, bona fide, to settle in the West," which, with the passing of covered-wagon days, has come down to nothing more romantic than operating a Travelers Aid center in the St. Louis railroad station.

The first foundation of the modern type, with broad social aims and few restrictions on the use of its money, was the Peabody Education Fund, established in 1867 with a $2,000,000 gift by George Peabody, a prescient banker of London and Baltimore, whose bust is in the Hall of Fame on University Heights. Peabody's hope was to repair some of the ravages of the Civil War, and his Fund, which had perhaps as able a board and staff as any foundation has ever boasted, did magnificent work in improving education in the South, especially among Negroes. The Fund was liquidated fifty years later and the remaining cash was given away, in accordance with the wise and modest proviso of its creator, who believed that foundations don't improve with age. This self-effacing policy, though it has been widely praised by observers who have noted that elderly foundations tend to develop hardening of the bureaucratic arteries, has been imitated by only one important foundation—the Julius Rosenwald Fund, which was also, coincidentally, devoted to Negro education, and which went out of business in 1948, after thirty years of activity that, among other things, stimulated the building of over 5,000 schools for Negroes in the South.

The golden, heroic age of American philanthropy was inaugurated and dominated by Andrew Carnegie and John D. Rockefeller, who were as bold and imaginative in the spending of their money as they had been in the making of it, and considerably more scrupulous. In 1889, Carnegie published his article on "the gospel of wealth," with its celebrated thesis, "The man who dies rich dies disgraced." One of the most enthusiastic fan letters he received came from Rockefeller, who wrote, "I would that more men of wealth were doing as you are doing with your money, but, be assured, your example will bear fruits, and the time will come when men of wealth will more generally be willing to use it for the good of others." The two millionaires went on to practice what they preached. Around 1900, Carnegie, prompted by the late John Shaw Billings, director of the New York Public Library, offered to build a public library for any English-speaking community in the world that would contribute, as a maintenance fund, ten per cent of the building's cost; by 1919 this rash offer had produced 2,811 libraries—about half of them in England and the British Empire—which cost him a total of $60,000,000. Rockefeller began with a small Baptist college, on which he spent an ultimate $35,000,000 to make it one of the great American universities—the University of Chicago. Presently, Carnegie and Rockefeller began to spawn foundations. Carnegie established the Carnegie Institution of Washington, devoted to scientific research, in 1902; the Carnegie Foundation for the Advancement of Teaching, in 1905; the Carnegie Endowment for International Peace, in 1910; and the Carnegie Corporation of New York, for just about everything, in 1911. Rockefeller founded the Rockefeller Institute for Medical Research in 1901; the General Education Board in 1903; the Rockefeller Sanitary Commission in 1909; the Rockefeller Foundation in 1913; and the Laura Spelman Rockefeller Memorial, devoted to social work and social sciences, in 1918.

The Rockefeller agencies made medical history with such exploits as their worldwide campaigns to control malaria and yellow fever, and their detection—and subsequent elimination—of hookworm as a drain on the vitality of rural Southerners. Carnegie money began the first nationwide system of pensions for college teachers and also financed Abraham Flexner's famous report, *Medical Education in the United States and Canada*, which appeared in 1910. After personally inspecting the hundred and fifty-five medical schools in both countries, Flexner found that three-fourths of them were completely inadequate and that only one—Johns Hopkins—was comparable to the great European schools. Rockefeller's General Education Board then took on Flexner and, with the Rockefeller Foundation, spent $100,000,000 on a reform program ($600,000,000 more was raised from other sources in the course of carrying it out) that in a few years created a number of first-rate medical schools, drove out of business some seventy-five institutions that were little more than diploma mills, and is generally credited with revolutionizing medical education in this country. Flexner's original report cost the Carnegie Corporation just $14,000, and stands as a classic example of a small grant's producing big results.

By the twenties, the golden age had begun to degenerate into the present silver age. In recent years, although the great foundations have not decreased their rate of spending, they have found it increasingly difficult to make the same splash with their money. The philanthropic frontier has been steadily closing as the government has taken over more and more of the fields that were pioneered by private enterprise. Public health and medical research have for quite some time now been financed in the main by government money; large areas that had formerly been served by private charity were appropriated by the New Deal; since the Second World War, the government has become by far the most substantial supporter of research in the physical sciences and, under its Fulbright Scholarship program, has sent more Americans to study in foreign

countries than all the foundations together have in the
past fifty years. (With his unerring instinct for a false
issue, Senator McCarthy has recently been sniping at the
Fulbright program, one of the few, if not indeed the only,
bright, original, and useful ideas our government has had
in many years. Luckily, the Senator's voice no longer has
the carrying power it once had. The New York *Times*,
for example, only gave the story four inches on page 13.)

Before the war, the government was spending about
$90,000,000 a year on scientific research and development;
now, stepping up the tempo from millions to billions, it is
spending $2,100,000,000 (largely on sciences related to
weapon development). Some $150,000,000 of the total goes
to universities for government-sponsored projects; trivial
though this sum is in comparison to what the government
is spending directly, it is more than all the foundations
combined contribute to university research. The Department of Commerce now undertakes the national-debt
surveys that were initiated by Edward A. Filene's Twentieth Century Fund, as well as much of the statistical
work on national income that was originally done by the
Rockefeller-financed National Bureau of Economic Research; the General Education Board's farm and home programs have long since become part of the Department of
Agriculture's extension service; and the Point Four program dispatches American experts and techniques to backward countries on a scale that no foundation can begin
to match.

Not only have the foundations been overshadowed by
the sheer size of government spending, but basic needs of
the kind they once met either no longer exist—partly as a
result of their own success—or are now considered the
rightful province of public funds. In this silver age, therefore, most of them have developed a policy of either going
in for retail trade—small grants for marginal projects—or,
when they do spend large amounts, giving the money to

established institutions. Their millions, in short, merely lubricate the gears of the status quo. In the jargon of the trade, they have become "discipline-oriented," which means that they first decide what "disciplines"—medicine, physics, economics, sociology, and so on—they believe need help, and then spend their money accordingly. But the Ford Foundation is "problem-oriented," as were the Carnegie and Rockefeller foundations in the golden age; it first decides on a problem that it thinks needs attention—the inroads on civil liberties within this country, say, or the gains of the Soviet bloc outside it—and then finances projects in the "disciplines" relevant to that problem. As the research director of the Reece Committee complained, "[The Ford Foundation] gives ample evidence of having taken the initiative in selecting purposes of its own. . . . It is the first foundation to dedicate itself openly to 'problem-solving' on a world scale." (Which is somehow reminiscent of Westbrook Pegler's description of Paul Hoffman as someone who "frankly describes himself in 'Who's Who' as a 'foundation executive.'")

In its adventurous spirit, in its readiness to experiment with large sums, and in its preference for creating its own agencies to solve the problems it is interested in (it has set up no fewer than eight autonomous funds, at least three of them with annual budgets larger than those of all but the very biggest foundations), the Ford Foundation is a throw-back to the golden age of Carnegie and Rockefeller, although whether its accomplishments will be as solid as theirs is as yet far from clear. There is no denying that since March, 1953, when Hoffman was succeeded as president by Gaither, the Foundation has become more cautious and that in a few years it may become indistinguishable, except in size, from its brothers. But it takes time to change the personality of a big institution, and the differences between Ford and the other large foundations are still marked.

CHAPTER **4**

WHAT HATH FORD WROUGHT!

A<small>LTHOUGH</small> the Ford Foundation was established in the middle thirties, it was almost entirely a local Detroit charity until Paul Hoffman became its president early in 1951. During the next four years, through 1954, it made grants totalling $186,000,000. In this chapter, which describes and evaluates in detail the Foundation's activities, we shall be concerned mostly with its 1951–1954 spending. Of the $186,000,000 total, some $89,000,000, or almost half, went for education; $54,000,000 for international programs; $15,000,000 to establish the Fund for the Republic, which is concerned with civil liberties; $8,000,000 for work in what the Foundation calls "the behavioral sciences," an extensive field that takes in sociology, psychology, economics, political science, anthropology, and pretty much whatever else anyone wants it to take in; $10,000,000 for economic development and administration; and the remaining $10,000,000 mostly for a miscellany of good works in the Detroit area.

Until last year, when the Ford Foundation itself began putting money into education, practically all its spending in this field was done by two specially created agencies— the Fund for the Advancement of Education, which had received $57,000,000 by the end of 1954, and the Fund for Adult Education, which had received $30,000,000. Although these two great Funds, which, like their parent, have offices on Madison Avenue, are commonly thought to be subsidiaries of the Foundation—when they are not, indeed, confused with it—actually they are wholly separate and self-governing, each having its own directors and its own staff.

The Fund for the Advancement of Education

The Fund for the Advancement of Education, which was set up in 1951 and has been spending about $6,-000,000 a year since then, or more than all but three or four other foundations spend, is frankly out to reform education as well as to advance it. "The support of new and experimental programs" is its announced major aim. The Fund sprang, full-grown, from the fertile and Olympian brow of Robert Maynard Hutchins while he was an associate director of the Foundation, and its activities bear a strong family resemblance to Dr. Hutchins' iconoclastic policies during his twenty-two years as head of the University of Chicago. At the outset, the Fund's board of directors was headed by Frank W. Abrams, chairman of the board of Standard Oil of New Jersey; he was succeeded by the late Owen J. Roberts, a former Supreme Court Justice; and the post is currently held by Roy E. Larsen, president of Time, Inc. The Fund's president is Dr. Clarence H. Faust, who was Dean of the College at the University of Chicago under Hutchins and more recently Director of Library Studies at Stanford. Up to this year, the Fund has spent $28,000,000, or about half of what it has received from the Foundation. Some $11,000,000 has gone into its most popular program —providing high-school and college teachers with fellowships whose charm is that they are given not for research or for "projects" but simply to allow a year off, with pay and expense money, for study, travel, or whatever else the recipients think will make them better teachers. The remaining $17,000,000 has gone mostly into experiment and innovation, notably the so-called Fifth-Year Program (over $6,000,000 up to 1956). The theory behind the Program is one that has long been a favorite of Hutchins—that our teachers have more know-how about teaching than knowledge of the subjects they teach because they get too much professional and too little general education; prospective teachers have to carry so heavy a load of vocational courses that they often don't get as broad a humanistic education as prospective dentists and salesmen do. Under the Program, future teachers take a regular four-year liberal-arts course, and to this is added a fifth year, in which they receive all their vocational training, combining study with part-time teaching, much as medical internes combine study with hospital work. The Program was originally called the Arkansas Plan, because it began in that state, all of whose fifteen colleges have gone into it. Outside Arkansas, eight colleges now participate, including Wayne, Temple, Goucher, Yale, and Harvard. The Fund's $6,-000,000 has been used to strengthen liberal-arts departments where necessary—as was the case in Arkansas—but mostly to underwrite the extra expenses of the fifth year for the colleges and for those students who could otherwise not afford it. The close-knit hierarchy of professional educators has welcomed this easy access to the mysteries of teaching about as enthusiastically as the Roman augurs would have welcomed a proposal to simplify the interpretation of entrails. The American Association of Colleges for Teacher Education at first denounced the Program as "an eighteenth-century model," and other educators have seen in it "a return to the middle ages." (Later, the Association backtracked far enough to recommend that prospective teachers get more general education than they do now.) The Fund has a trump card, however, in the rapidly

growing shortage of schoolteachers caused by the unexpected rise in the postwar birth rate. In 1954, there was
a deficit of 162,000 teachers, and the school population
is expected to grow annually, at least through 1960. Obviously, if only a limited amount of professional training
is required, more college graduates with unspecialized degrees can go into teaching.

The Fifth-Year Program is not the only experiment in
which the Fund has capitalized on the providential coincidence of virtue and necessity. Thus, its "pre-induction
scholarships" ($3,000,000 to 1956), which every year en-
able several hundred especially gifted students to skip the
last two years of high school and enter college, are a
response to two current problems—the pressure on the
schools and the cutting short of college by the draft—as
well as an echo of a Hutchins policy at Chicago. The
Fund has also engaged in a number of other activities, such
as giving $300,000 to the Portland, Oregon, Board of
Education for the purpose of making its public schools
more interesting to bright youngsters; experimenting
with television as one way to use the limited supply of
teachers more effectively; providing teachers in the
schools of Bay City, Michigan, and Fairfield, Connecticut, with classroom aides who do the "housekeeping"
chores, like taking the roll, dictating spelling tests, and
correcting papers, and so enable each teacher to handle
more pupils; making grants to between thirty and forty
colleges for surveys of their business management methods
and educational aims; financing a study of how the last two
years of high school can be better-integrated with the first
two years of college (another Hutchinsian echo); and
financing studies of racial desegregation in schools. When
the Fund was first started, someone sourly observed that
"Hutchins is trying to buy what he couldn't sell." The
witticism seems strained. For one thing, some of Hutchins'
main ideas—such as his advocacy of more humanistic and

fewer "service-station," or vocational, college courses and his conservative counter-revolution against the extremes to which some progressive educators have carried John Dewey's theories—were by no means his alone, although he expressed them more provocatively than others did. Also, the Fund's program as it has worked out in practice involves a good deal more than the Hutchins doctrine.

One of the most fascinating, though possibly not the most important, investments made by the Fund for the Advancement of Education is the $640,000 it has put into the Institute for Philosophical Research, which is headed by Dr. Mortimer J. Adler, one of Hutchins' old comrades-in-arms in the intellectual wars at the University of Chicago and, more recently, co-editor with him of the Encyclopædia Britannica's $298 set of Great Books. "We wanted to achieve clarity about the functions of education," explains President Faust of the Fund. "This involved us in a consideration of the nature of man and society. The grant was given to work out the basic problems." More (or possibly less) specifically, Dr. Adler's Institute announced its aim as being a "dialectical examination of Western humanistic thought, with a view to providing assistance in the clarification of basic philosophical and educational issues in the modern world."

At the beginning, in 1952, Dr. Adler talked in terms of a *"Summa Dialectica"* of modern thought, comparable to Thomas Aquinas' *Summa Theologica* of medieval thought, and set the year 2002 as the final deadline for its completion. After three years of operation, during which he and his eighteen associates became sadder if not wiser, Dr. Adler conceded that "sober second thoughts, born of experience" (always unsettling to a dialectician), indicate that "it is not necessary, nor is it sound, to think of the whole encyclopedic work as something to be done by any one organization"—and one can see his point in view of the fact that, after spending three years and some $600,000, the Institute has got around to only one aspect of Western humanistic thought. This is embodied in a two-volume mimeographed work entitled *Research on Freedom: Report of Dialectical Discoveries and Constructions (from May 1953 to October 1954)*. The production, of which one volume is bibliography, lives up to its title. It is a jungle of jargon, a Luna Park of "nuclear agreements," "taxonomic questions," "explicative issues," and "general issues"—all of them classified and subdivided in a logical framework of Rube Goldbergian complexity. There is food for thought on every page—in fact, a whole winter's supply. To quote at random: "We have discovered simply as a matter of fact that if an author does subscribe to two nuclear agreements, he will disagree with an author who subscribes to only one of these two, in a way that is different from the way in which authors who subscribe to only one disagree among themselves." Toward the end of the first, or non-bibliographical, volume, the authors begin to suspect that their attempt to treat ideas like species of beetles, capable of being scientifically classified (pinned down, so to speak), is too great for the capacities of the English language. "Problems of style [are] most vexatious," they confess. "The language we have invented in order to reach a common understanding of our primary notions is, unfortunately, a 'private language,' consisting of the special words and symbols we had to employ to facilitate strictly intramural communication. [We must] invent a perspicuous and effective literary format for the communication of our findings." How far from such an invention they still are is indicated by their use of the word "perspicuous," which is an unclear word for "clear." President Faust, however, expresses no disappointment in the results, and is looking forward to reading *Research on Freedom: Report of Dialectical Discoveries and Constructions* in an English translation, to prepare which his Fund has given Dr. Adler's Institute a "terminal grant" of $75,000. The inference to be drawn from this last fact depends on whether one emphasizes "terminal" or "grant."

The Fund for Adult Education

The Fund for Adult Education, another legacy of the Hoffman-Hutchins regime, is an enterprise of almost indescribable ambition, complexity, and vagueness. Its chairman is Clarence Francis, who was formerly chairman of General Foods, and its president is C. Scott Fletcher, who has been closely associated with Hutchins and Hoffman; he was at one time president of Encyclopædia Britannica Films, which, like the Britannica itself, is owned chiefly by the University of Chicago, and, before that, he was sales manager of the Studebaker Corporation, when Hoffman was its president. The Fund aims at nothing less than the development of "mature, wise, and responsible citizens who can participate intelligently in a free society." In pursuance of this great end, it had spent $25,000,000 by the fall of 1955. About a third went into educational television and radio—a Center has been established at Ann Arbor, Michigan, to prepare and distribute programs to radio and television stations; grants have been made to groups in Boston, Pittsburgh, St. Louis, San Francisco, and other communities for the construction of educational TV stations; and organizations like the National Association of Educational Broadcasters have been encouraged by cash donations, or—in the chaste usage of foundations—"supporting grants." The remaining two-thirds of the Fund's expenditures have gone for a variety of things but essentially for one general purpose—to induce people to meet regularly in small groups to study and discuss world affairs, politics, economics, and the humanities. The Fund provides the money for various institutions to supply "study aids" in the form of books, pamphlets, records, and motion-picture films; underwrites fellowships; sends organizers out to work with community leaders; and helps support the Adult Education Association, which is the trade organization of professionals engaged in that field. Above all, the Fund makes generous grants to a score of organizations that are concerned with educating adults, ranging alphabetically from the American Foundation for Political Education (whose "Discussion Groups in World Politics" have received $756,000, second only to the $826,000 given to one of Hutchins' pet causes, the Great Books Foundation) to the University of Chicago, which has received grants to make films entitled "Room for Discussion," "How to Organize a Discussion Group," and "How to Conduct a Discussion Group."

Adult education has been with us for over a century. The idea used to be self-improvement with a view to making more money; there were the mechanics' institutes of Victorian England, the courses in "word-power" and "memory-building" ("Mr. Addison Sims, of Seattle! I remember you perfectly!"), and the Harvard Classics, whose Fifteen Minutes a Day would enable one to impress the boss at dinner with easy allusions to Thucydides. Now, in our more socially conscious age, the emphasis is on making better citizens. To accomplish this, the Fund employs a distinctively American combination of organization at the top and anarchy at the bottom. Anybody can join an adult-education group and—in theory, at least—be listened to politely, regardless of race, creed, color, or previous condition of platitude. The job of the group leader, like that of a progressive-school teacher, is to "bring out" the members, not to instruct them from expert knowledge. The object, according to the Fund, is "the stimulation of basic curiosity, imagination, and the habit of critical thought, as opposed to the passive acceptance of ready-made opinions." But the topic under discussion at any given meeting has usually been decided on in advance and handed down from above—by the American Foundation for Political Education, the Great Books Foundation, or whatever organization has worked up that particular program—and the material to be studied has been predigested and packaged at headquarters and sent out to the group in the form of specially prepared textbooks, essays, bibliographies, study guides, films, and records. The discussion leaders are primed with elaborate how-to manuals and lists of "stimulating" questions along these lines: "Our essayist points out that the average farm in India is not over five acres and that it consists of several scattered pieces. To what extent can modern agricultural methods be introduced under these conditions? Do you see any way of attacking the problem?"

Optimism about the ability of Des Moines housewives and Little Rock doctors to grapple with such issues is oddly combined with skepticism about their acquiring knowledge on their own hook, without benefit of guidance and encouragement from headquarters. The theory is that high-powered methods are necessary to compete for people's leisure time against the movies, television, sports, popular magazines, and other forms of mass entertainment. It may be true that the average American will not read and discuss seriously of his own accord but must be prodded and cajoled by much the same methods that are used by the commercial competitors for his spare time. But this kind of competition sometimes appears to be producing a merger in which education itself becomes just another aspect of our mass culture. As the consumer of Wheaties is coaxed to eat his morning bowlful by means of carefully prepared advertising and ingenious promotion, so the consumer of adult education is induced to drink—or anyway to sip—at the Pierian spring. Community "drives" are put on and leaflets and brochures, written in the breezy, "grassroots" lingo of the pitchman and pepped up by numerous little drawings of a mildly humorous flavor, are distributed in profusion. And, like the Wheaties customer, the adult educatee is closely studied, his penchants, whims, and aversions analyzed, and the best way to "approach" him is set forth in the trade journals of the movement. *This* road to learning is a royal one— a superhighway with overpasses to avoid the more difficult aspects of the subject, electronic devices to slow down intellectual hot-rodders, and tow trucks to keep the laggards in motion.

For all the planning and study, however, nobody has yet come up with a satisfactory answer to the question: How much are the students getting out of it? The least that can be said of these lay seminars is that no harm is done and the participants have an innocuously enjoyable time. From the most sanguine point of view, the students really do become better-informed citizens. But since there are no marks, no examinations, no standards beyond "democratic participation," and no penalties for not doing one's homework, there is no way to measure results. The Fund has reported that in its first year it "devoted considerable time to a comprehensive stock-taking of the bewildering array of existing adult-educational activities and agencies." The results of the stock-taking seem to have bewildered the Fund itself. At least, it has been more guilty than any other part of the Ford Foundation of what Frederick T. Gates, the elder Rockefeller's adviser in philanthropy, called "scatteration"—the spreading of a lot of small grants over a wide area instead of effectively concentrating on a few carefully chosen objectives.

A joint committee of the Fund and its parent Foundation recently completed another exploration of its field— or, rather, morass—with the aim of achieving some "evaluations" and of drawing jurisdictional lines between the Fund's interests and the Foundation's. President Fletcher of the Fund, a salesman type, preferred to describe the process as "deciding areas of emphasis." But however one describes the committee's deliberations, there can be no doubt as to their results. The Fund for Adult Education

will never be the same again. The Foundation has cut it off
with a mere $3,500,000 a year for the next five years—
about half the standard of living to which it had become
accustomed. ("The new grant," explained Mr. Fletcher,
"will be used to continue an even more concentrated program to help adults develop those powers of critical thinking and responsible action necessary for both successful
personal life and good citizenship." By "more concentrated" Mr. Fletcher apparently means "smaller.") Furthermore, the Foundation will subsidize directly, and not
through the Fund, the radio-and-television Center at Ann
Arbor, which was perhaps the Fund's most important
single activity.

All of this hardly adds up to a vote of confidence, especially when a third conclusion of the committee is considered, namely, that the most fruitful field for future sub-
sidies is the promotion not of those discussion groups which
the Fund has hitherto promoted, but rather of extension
courses in regular colleges and universities. In short, the
committee seems to have felt some dissatisfaction with the
concrete results from the $25,000,000 President Fletcher
has to date scattered over the misty landscape of adult
education, and to have attempted to scramble back onto
terra firma. It is not the first time something of the sort
has happened. In the twenties and thirties, the Carnegie
Corporation spent a lot of money on adult education, but
it finally concluded that the results didn't justify further
investment. Perhaps the only safe generalization on the
subject is one from the Fund's 1951 report: "Adult-education activities are largely non-institutional, sporadic, un-
coördinated, and highly varied."

International Programs

From 1951 through 1954, the Ford Foundation put
$54,000,000, or almost a third of its total outlay for the

period, into its international programs. Ford is the most globally conscious of the large foundations, partly because it began its heavy spending during the Korean war, when the threat of Communist expansion seemed most acute, partly because the internationally minded Paul Hoffman was then its head, and partly because Henry Ford II, who has been its chairman all along, is more aware than many other businessmen of the existence of the rest of the world. Rockefeller spends about the same proportion of its budget overseas, but—as might be expected of a discipline-oriented foundation—mostly for scientific research in universities. Ford, on the other hand, being problem-oriented—the problem here is how to win allies and influence neutrals— is less interested in research per se than in promoting sympathy and understanding between us and the rest of the non-Communist world. (Strange to say, our most violent anti-Communists are also the most critical of the Foundation for its "globalism," a familiar paradox of American political reasoning.)

The Foundation's international programs have been of three kinds: first, financing refugee work, plus furthering the exchange of ideas and persons between America and the rest of the world; second, encouraging and financing the study of foreign nations by American scholars and laymen; and, third and most important, aiding "overseas development," which means giving money to local institutions abroad and introducing American technology and "know-how" to backward countries.

In the first category, the Foundation's two biggest efforts in the field of refugee work are now past history—$3,000,-000 to fifteen private agencies, working through the United Nations' High Commissioner for Refugees, with the object of reaching "a final solution of the refugee problem in Europe," and $4,000,000 to the East European Fund, an agency the Foundation created in 1951 to help the 100,000 exiles from Soviet nations who have come to this country since 1945. The East European Fund supported a Community Integration Program to help these refugees get settled in Boston, New York, Buffalo, Los Angeles, and six other cities; it set up a Research Program on the U.S.S.R., which employed Soviet exiles to write a vast number of monographs, on everything from *Soviet Peat Resources* (201 pp., $3.75) to *Logic and Dialectic in the Soviet Union* (89 pp., $1.25), not excluding *Kalmyk Secondary Education in the 1930s, The Soviet View of Reflexology*, and *The* Nasha Niva *Group, 1906–1917: A Study of the Origins of Modern Byelorussian Cultural Nationalism;* and it founded the Chekhov Publishing House, which has become the leading Russian-language publisher outside the Soviet Union, putting out works by exiles, translations, and Russian classics. The Foundation, however, has recently announced a "terminal" grant, and Chekhov will go out of existence unless it can find support elsewhere.

The Foundation continues to promote the exchange of ideas and people. An example of the first is its support of an internationally distributed cultural quarterly, *Perspectives USA*. An example of the second is the annual grant to the 4-H Clubs, which the Clubs use to send several dozen American farm boys and girls to work for three months on farms in Burma, Iran, India, Israel, Jordan, Lebanon, Nepal, Pakistan, Syria, and Turkey and to bring youths here from those countries to live and work with American farm families. Ford's latest big exchange-of-persons program is the Lafayette Fellowship Foundation, set up in 1955 with a $1,000,000 appropriation, which will be used to bring ten French students over each year for two years of study in the United States.

The Foundation's efforts to make Americans more sophisticated about other countries have been heroic. In 1954, sixty-five Ford Fellows were somewhere East of Suez. The Foundation spends about $1,000,000 a year on fellowships for study of the Near and Far East, the U.S.S.R., Eastern Europe, and Africa. It has enabled the Rice Institute, of Houston, Texas, to dispatch a team of sociologists to the Near East to study the psychological conflicts of adolescents, the idea being that since adolescents are the least stable age group, they will show most clearly the strains that backward cultures undergo in their efforts to adjust to Western influences. On the domestic scene, it has financed, among other projects, a series of African studies at Northwestern, Howard, and Boston Universities, and a study of political life in Indonesia at Cornell. It has given the Greater New York Council for Foreign Students $10,000 "for the study of the adjustments of foreign students in the New York area." (There are now 34,000 such students in this country, and the *Village Voice*, a new Greenwich Village weekly, recently reported that over 1,500 of them settled in New York south of Thirty-fourth Street between June and October of 1955.) It has subsidized the American Council of Learned Societies to prepare, for use by students in the United States, readers and dictionaries written in various Asiatic languages that are spoken by at least 500,000,000 people and that include such tongues as Pushtu, Amoy, Wu. Lao, Sindhi, Marathi, Uzbec, Karen, Uigur (or Wigor), and Telugu. (Paul Harvey, a radio commentator on ABC, denounced the Telugu dictionary as a typical Ford globaldoggle: "Telugu . . . is a neglected Oriental language. . . . If the disturbed dead could turn in their graves, old Henry would be whirling tonight." He was apparently unaware that 30,000,000 Indians speak the language and that Moscow's propagandists, who have put out a Russian-Telugu dictionary, are regularly sending printed material written in Telugu into India.) The Foundation tries to reach the serious-minded layman through outfits like the Council on Foreign Relations, to which it gave $1,500,000 last year for research and education in international problems; it also subsidizes a string of learned journals, including *African Abstracts*, the *Far Eastern Quarterly*, the *Journal of Central European Affairs*, and *Middle East Research Reports*.

The Foundation's overseas-development programs are limited to the Near and Far East. This is partly because the Soviet influence is strongest there. It is also because, as Don Price, the vice-president who has had the most to do with these programs, puts it, "Something like a quarter of the world's population has become independent since World War Two, and anything we can do to help it get settled on a basis of free government and economic progress will be a good thing. The belt of new countries we are working with would have tremendous problems even if there were no such thing as Communism." The cynic would stress only the anti-Soviet motivation, but a cynic cannot wholly understand the Ford Foundation; the sense of philanthropic duty expressed by Mr. Price may well play as large a part in the Foundation's behavior as the less elevated motives the cynic specializes in.

The Foundation's overseas spending is, of course, tiny compared to that of the United States government, which, for instance, gives India $85,000,000 in non-military aid a year, as opposed to the Foundation's $3,000,000 or so. But the latter can experiment more freely with its money than can government agencies accountable to Congress. The Foundation's first big program in India, agreed on in the summer of 1951 at a conference between Foundation President Hoffman and Premier Nehru, consisted of sending hundreds of Indian social workers into some 1,500 villages to try to interest the peasants in all sorts of basic skills long familiar in the West but still largely unknown in the East— crop rotation, planting seeds in rows (instead of by the more picturesque broadcast method), making and using better implements (merely putting an iron tip on the traditional wooden plowshare means a big increase in production), irrigation, road building, sanitation, the use of fertilizers, and, for the women, modern methods of cooking, sewing, and hygiene. The response was enthusiastic, the program successful, and now that it has emerged from the experimental stage, it is being extended throughout rural India by the Nehru regime with the help of American government funds.

Ford money, indeed, is changing things all over the East. In Turkey, it has enabled the government to set up an Institute of Business Administration in Istanbul and a library school in Ankara. The Institute of Business Administration, in which the Harvard Business School and some forty Turkish firms are also involved, may put an end to contretemps of the sort that occurred recently when the new Hilton hotel in Istanbul had to buy its furnishings—except, presumably, its rugs—outside Turkey, because no native manufacturer could or would turn out Western-style furniture in quantity. The library school was started because in 1953 there were only two trained librarians in Turkey; in most libraries the books were—and to a large extent still are—indexed and arranged not by subject but by date of acquisition or, in more advanced ones, by author alone. A new project, for which the Foundation appropriated $500,-000 last year, the Southern Languages Book Trust, will attempt to compete with the flood of cheap books in the vernacular languages of southern India that is now being subsidized by Moscow; the Trust will distribute American and European titles chosen by a board that includes the vice-chancellors of seven Indian universities.

Concern about the welfare of Indian peasants and Turkish librarians is a new thing under the sun for a lot of Americans. "In more recent years, the recognition has grown that our own freedom and even our survival can now depend on happenings thousands of miles from our own shores," President Gaither wrote in the Foundation's statement to the Reece Committee. "Because of this recognition, the American people are carrying unprecedented burdens in an effort to establish a just peace throughout the world. In this effort, the Ford Foundation feels it can as a private agency play a small but significant role." Or, in less official terms, competition with an expanding Communist empire has caused some Americans to worry more than they used to about the rest of the world. To what curious lengths this has gone is illustrated by the story of the Ford Foundation's Pali Project, which also may serve as the case history of a grant.

On February 4, 1952, Abbot Low Moffat, head of the United States Technical and Economic Mission to Burma, wrote the Foundation's then President Hoffman that Premier Nu had asked for American help in creating an International Institute for Advanced Buddhistic Studies in Rangoon. Premier Nu, who was having a bad time with the local Communists (his predecessor, General Aung San, had been killed by their gunmen), was trying to strengthen Buddhism as the chief cultural heritage that his racially disunited people have in common. The Institute was to be completed during the Sixth Great Buddhist Council, which was scheduled to be held in Rangoon from Full Moon Day of May, 1954, to Full Moon Day of May, 1956, and which would be attended by Buddhist priests and scholars from all over Asia. Mr. Moffat enclosed a memorandum from Thado Maha Thray Sithu U Chan Htoon, Attorney General of Burma, explaining that only five Great Councils had been held since the death of Buddha, that the Council would end on the twenty-five-hundredth anniversary of that death (a year in which tradition had it that there would be a great revival of Buddhism), that the Burmese government was making a hundred acres of land available to the Council and spending forty lakhs of kyats ($800,-000) to erect buildings on it, which would later be converted into a permanent Buddhist University, and that the

University and the proposed adjacent Institute for Advanced Studies, or graduate school, were "expected to become the spiritual center of Southeast Asia, radiating such irresistible and overpowering rays of Wisdom, Truth, and Righteousness as would dispel from the earth those dark and evil forces rooted in Lobha (Greed), Dosa (Hatred), and Moha (Delusion), which are now threatening to swamp and swallow the whole of Asia and the world." The Burmese government was also planning to spend $600,000 on a new, definitive edition and translation —into Burmese—of the principal religious texts written in Pali, an ancient language that is to Buddhism much what Latin is to the Catholic Church. Most of the texts were on palm-leaf manuscripts, though some had been recorded on 789 marble slabs by the Fifth Great Buddhist Council, which met in Mandalay in 1871. One thing the Institute was needed for was to house the texts and the scholars working on them. Mr. Moffat ended his letter by saying that Premier Nu felt that "the popular belief that Americans work solely for the material benefit of themselves or others is one of the strongest weapons in the hands of Communist propagandists in Southeast Asia." Since the American mission was unable to finance the Institute—the use of government funds to promote heathenism being thought politically inexpedient—perhaps the Ford Foundation could step into the breach? Within a few days, President Hoffman got another letter urging support of the Pali Project, from Edwin G. Arnold, who was then director of the Far East Program of the Mutual Security Agency and is now on the Foundation's staff.

Six months later, after two Foundation executives had returned from Burma with a favorable report, President Hoffman wrote Premier Nu that the Pali Project was being sympathetically considered. Before long, he wrote again to say that Dr. John Scott Everton, president of Kalamazoo College, in Michigan, had taken an extended leave of absence to represent the Foundation in Burma. (Dr. Everton is still in Rangoon, working for the Foundation and, on the side, teaching a course in American philosophy at Rangoon University.) On April 5, 1953, Dr. Everton reported that after talking with U Win, Minister for National Planning and Religious Affairs, he thought the Pali Project should include a library building, trained librarians, books and microfilmed manuscripts, and a teaching staff. That fall, the Foundation wrote U Win that a grant of $250,000 had been voted by the trustees, to which the Minister replied, "Many thanks."

Presently, the Delhi architectural firm of Polk & Mehandru was engaged; Dr. Niharranjan Ray, a distinguished Indian scholar and a Ghosh Fellow of Calcutta University, was commissioned to train librarians; and two Burmese scholars, U Hpe Aung and U Hla Maung, were brought over to observe library practices in this country and to study at the Columbia Library School. (U Hpe Aung had taken his M.A. at the University of Rangoon in 1951, with a thesis on "Clarification and Critical Analysis of the Various Processes Involved in the Attainment of Lokiya-Samadhi through Samatha.") The usual problems arose. Dr. Ray wanted a car, which was granted on condition that it remain in Burma when he left; the building was delayed because the original contractor had to be fired and because the monsoon rains came early and stopped construction; and Premier Nu had a vision in a dream that obliged the architects to revise their plans in such a way as to introduce Buddhist symbols and other changes of a religious rather than a functional nature. Moreover, bringing over U Hpe Aung and U Hla Maung was complex and expensive, as such operations usually are. The total cost came to some $21,000, which went mainly for their living expenses ($11,200), plane tickets ($4,300), tuition ($3,-500), and a fee of $950 to the Institute of International Education for arranging it all. But things worked out in the end, also as usual. In July, 1954, Dr. Ray's library school graduated twelve students, with impressive ceremonies; the Messrs. Aung and Maung did well at Columbia, having studied diligently (though possibly not so diligently as three other students, who were recently sent there by the government of a small Asiatic country and were told before leaving home that the penalty for not getting their degrees would be decapitation). The Institute was completed this spring. It is modern in style, and will be air-conditioned, to prevent the books from mildewing. (Rangoon has ninety-nine inches of rainfall a year.) As for the Sixth Council, it began on schedule on Full Moon Day of 1954, which that year was May 17th. Dr. Everton responded to his invitation to the ceremonies with a printed letter, in English, quoting appropriate Buddhist verses and closing, "We of the Ford Foundation join you in one common prayer for the well-being of all sentient beings." The Council has been convening in an atmosphere something like that of a Midwestern barn-raising. The 15,000 Buddhist monks and scholars who came from all over the East to attend it have been fed in open-air canteens run by committees of ladies, including the wives of high government officials. Sessions were held in two huge structures—a World Peace Pagoda and a central assembly hall, the outside of which was covered with earth and stones by Premier Nu and other volunteer workers in consequence of a vision he had that the Council should meet in a cave. When it ended this spring, after a mere two years, the Sixth Council had made a moderate showing compared to that of the Fourth, which sat for sixteen years—from 29 to 13 B.C.

The Fund for the Republic

The Fund for the Republic has been described by its president, Robert M. Hutchins, as "a wholly disowned subsidiary of the Ford Foundation." The sour note is not unintentional. Neither the Fund nor the Foundation enjoys being confused with the other, as is constantly happening, despite the fact that the Foundation has no control over the Fund. Although the Foundation set up the Fund for the Republic in 1952 with a founding grant of $15,000,000, relations between the two have never been cordial, and there is no question of any further subsidies; the Fund plans to go out of business when its money is spent, which it hopes will be four or five years from now. "The Fund has no other axe to grind than the support of the traditional liberties of the American people," President Hutchins declares. Specifically, the Fund's aim is the defense of the first ten amendments to the Constitution of the United States, otherwise known as the Bill of Rights. This is a rather daring enterprise at present (the Chief Justice of the Supreme Court recently observed that he didn't think Congress would pass the Bill of Rights if it came up today), and nothing the Foundation has done has got it into so much hot water as its founding of the Fund for the Republic. The Fund's first action was bold to the point of foolhardiness—granting $25,000 to the American Bar Association to make a study of the uses and abuses of Congressional investigating committees. When this was announced, the press and commentators of the extreme Right at once began a violent campaign based on the attractive, though untrue, notion that the whole $15,000,000 was to be used "to investigate Congress" and comparing this sum to the mere $250,000 or so a year the Un-American Activities Committee and the McCarthy Committee had to scrape along on. The actual results of the study hardly justified all the excitement. In time, the American Bar Association issued its report, a densely legalistic 45-page document with an appendix of 166 pages, which was duly submitted for consideration to the appropriate government

WHAT HATH FORD WROUGHT!

agencies and may or may not have had some beneficial effect.

The Fund for the Republic has evolved at a majestically slow pace. It began in 1949, as a gleam in the eye of the Foundation's Study Committee, whose report on "Area II, The Strengthening of Democracy," started off:

The Foundation should support activities directed toward:
A. The elimination of restrictions on freedom of thought, inquiry, and expression in the United States, and the development of policies and procedures best adapted to protect these rights in the face of persistent international tension.

Two years later, the Foundation's trustees decided that Area II, Subhead A, should be implemented by a new agency, which, after another year of meditation, finally emerged in December, 1952, as the Fund for the Republic, with Hoffman as chairman. In some circles, the Fund is called "Paul Hoffman's severance pay," and it is true that Hoffman originally supported Hutchins in proposing it, that its establishment coincided with Hoffman's extrusion from the Foundation, and that his son, Hallock, is now assistant to President Hutchins. The Fund's elephantine gestation is perhaps explained by the dilemma of the Ford trustees, all eminent and respectable citizens, who found themselves being chivied by Hoffman and Hutchins into doing something that was as "controversial" as it was logical on the basis of the program they themselves had adopted. But even after the Fund had its own independent board, its progress continued to be glacierlike. In its first two years, it was able to spend only about $1,250,000 of its $15,000,000 bank roll. One trouble was that its directors—also, to a man, eminent and respectable—had a hard time finding someone to run it who was both a prominent Republican and an enthusiast for civil liberties. After offering the job to the then Governor of California, Earl

Warren, they finally settled on Clifford Case, a rising young congressman from New Jersey, who was both a Republican and a liberal—in that order, as it turned out. He accepted the presidency in May, 1953, delayed taking office until Congress adjourned in August, and then resigned the next March to campaign, successfully, for the Republican nomination for senator from New Jersey. In May, 1954, the slightly desperate directors offered the job to Hutchins, under whom things have moved faster. But the five-year delay between the Study Committee's first statement of the need for a counterattack on "restrictions on freedom of thought, inquiry, and expression" and Hutchins' appointment was particularly unfortunate because it was during just those years that the Bill of Rights was being most rapidly eroded. A McCarthy can go into action with a purloined letter or two, but a $15,000,000 operation like the Fund needs all sorts of studies, reports, conferences, and top-level soul-searching to get moving. By the fall of 1954, when Hutchins really began to spend money, the junior Senator from Wisconsin had fired his ringing shot against freedom and subsided. Too much and too late may be the epitaph of the Fund for the Republic.

The Fund's first two years were expensive as well as lethargic. It cost $410,000 in administrative expenses to spend $843,000 on grants and projects, which is to say that expenses came to a third of its total outlay. This is very high. In 1953, for example, Rockefeller's expenses were thirteen per cent of its total outlay and Carnegie's seven per cent. Ford's were either five per cent, if one figures them on the same basis as the others, or ten per cent, if one does not include the $35,000,000 that went in three huge chunks to the Fund for the Advancement of Education, the Fund for Adult Education, and the Fund for the Republic. The latter basis seems the more realistic, since the expense of giving out money in such gigantic sums is obviously not comparable to that of administering a large number of more normal-sized grants. The Fund's high expense rate is accounted for partly by the fact that it pays its fourteen directors an annual salary of $3,000 apiece, or $42,000 a year, for services that are rendered gratis in most foundations. Although the salary of the Fund's president, like that of President Gaither of the Foundation, has never been officially revealed, it has been estimated at $35,000. (Gaither's is probably around $50,-000.) In the light of these munificent emoluments and the facts that a new organization is expensive to run, that the Case fiasco didn't help, and that the Fund does itself well as to offices, expense accounts, and the like, it becomes fairly clear why the Fund had to spend one dollar on itself for every two it gave away. As for the money the Fund did manage to spend on actual work during its first two years, over half went into the more or less politically safe field of interracial relations. The most striking thing about civil liberties since 1945 has been the contrast between the gain in Negroes' rights and the loss in other kinds of civil liberties. "The Fund's directors have been overcautious, overconservative—for understandable reasons," a Ford Foundation trustee who has been close to the Fund observed not long ago. Under Hutchins, expenses have been cut to twenty per cent (which is still high) and less attention has been paid to defending Negroes, who have other champions, including the Supreme Court, and more to defending citizens under political attack, whose need for help is greater.

Politicians, foundations, and other organisms sensitive to unfavorable publicity go in heavily for "fact-finding" when they feel they are in danger of having to take the unpopular side of an issue. "Let's get the facts first, then we'll know where we stand" is a kind of stalling that appeals to the pragmatic American temper. Thus, in the pre-Hutchins period the Fund's biggest outlay, apart from its spending for racial equality, was a grant of $550,000 for a study of "Communist Influence in the United States." Conceived on the grandest academic scale, this was divided into three parts: a $186,000 Gallup-type poll on attitudes of Americans toward minority rights, whose results were recently published by its director, Professor Samuel A. Stouffer, a Harvard sociologist, as a book, *Communism, Conformity, and Civil Liberties;* a roundup, costing $64,-000, of data consisting of a microfilm record of important trials involving Communists, a bibliography of books and articles on American Communism, plus "a compilation of abstracts of decisions, laws, ordinances, hearings, reports, and other public documents" on the subject (1,200 copies of the bibliography and the abstracts, in two big volumes, have been given free to libraries, and about two hundred have been sold, at $10 a set); and an analysis of "Communist Influence in Major Segments of United States Society," which is now being prepared by twelve learned individuals, in as many volumes, under the direction of Professor Clinton Rossiter, of Cornell, at a cost of $300,000. When it is all completed, "the facts" about American Communism may or may not have been adequately put on record. (The bibliography has been severely criticized for omitting many important articles written by the more sophisticated critics of Communism and for including a vast amount of trivia from the Party press, and Professor Rossiter, who was partly responsible for the job, has announced that it will be revised.) But there will still remain to be accomplished "the support of the traditional liberties of the American people."

Hutchins makes fun of his former colleagues in the Ford Foundation because their first reaction to the idea of establishing the Fund for the Republic was to propose a fact-finding commission. "I took the position that such a commission was not necessary," he recalls, adding dryly, "I was finally able to persuade them of this." Hutchins says that action is what is needed—"We are not interested in long-term scholarly research"—but his practice is weaker than his preaching. From the start, the Fund declined to take on individual defense cases, thereby casting an academic pallor over itself, and Hutchins has continued this policy, giving the excuse that the American Civil Liberties Union already does the job. Moreover, some of the projects initiated under him seem as "long-term scholarly" as any in the previous administration. During his presidency, for example, the Fund has appropriated $150,000 for "Fear in Education—A study of attitudes of college and high-school teachers," an exercise in "questionnaire sociology" that is being directed by Paul Lazarsfeld, of Columbia, and which will probably have the same practical effects as last year's investigation into attitudes toward minority rights, by Dr. Lazarsfeld's confrere, Dr. Stouffer, has had to date, namely none; $106,700 "for research and planning of a study of Right Wing extremist groups"; $25,000 for "exploration of a continuing agency to appraise the performance of the media of mass communication"; $9,000 "for a preliminary exploration of the right to publish and read" by the National Book Committee; and $7,000 for "a conspectus on civil liberties," which was requested by the Fund's directors for their own enlightenment.

On the other hand, under Hutchins the Fund has moved into a number of livelier, and often more perilous, areas, in which research is a tool for social action rather than an academic perquisite. It is spending $340,000 to encourage television shows on civil-liberties themes; $100,000 on the first full-dress study of political blacklisting—the "Red Channels" kind of thing—in the movies, radio, and TV; $150,000 to help the American Friends Service Committee, a Quaker group, provide legal defense for conscientious objectors; $115,000 on fellowships and grants-in-aid to individuals working "in areas of the Fund's interest"; $100,000 to enable the New York Bar Association's Special

Committee on the Federal Loyalty-Security Program to investigate the government's loyalty program; $100,000 for a research project on the same topic, the first fruit of which was a compilation of case histories, by Adam Yarmolinsky (he is now the Fund's representative in Washington, D.C.), that made the front pages last summer; $47,500 to further the Common Council for American Unity's work in protecting the legal rights of aliens, especially in deportation cases; $35,000 for "a study of Post Office interference with the flow of information and opinion"; and $25,000 for an analysis by the Stanford Law School of the testimony of government witnesses in cases involving Communism.

Such activities, as might be expected, have had a stimulating effect on various people, notably on Fulton Lewis, Jr., who since last August has been staging a radio marathon on the iniquities of the Fund (with sideswipes at its parent Foundation every now and then), devoting almost every one of his programs, five nights a week, to the subject; on Seaborn P. Collins, Jr., the outgoing National Commander of the American Legion, who urged the 1955 convention to boycott the Fund as a menace to national security (no action was taken); and on Attorney General Brownell, for whom the Fund has woven a hair shirt consisting of the Stanford inquiry into government witnesses, the $200,000 double look into the federal loyalty program, and an article by Richard H. Rovere on paid government witnesses in Communist cases, "The Kept Witnesses," which was originally commissioned by the Fund as part of a larger, and stillborn, project, and which the author finally published in *Harper's* (the Fund sent out 25,000 reprints to its mailing list).

The effect of all this on Hutchins, who dreads controversy as Br'er Rabbit dreaded the briar patch, seems to have been slight. Last fall, he was questioned for hours at a press conference by predominantly hostile reporters. He gave no visible ground, and even occupied a new and dangerously exposed outpost: He not only defended the Fund's recent hiring for a short period of a former Communist who had just "taken the Fifth" before a Congressional committee but went so far as to say, "I wouldn't hesitate to hire a Communist for a job he was qualified to do, provided I was in a position to see he did it." He added later that he thought a man's Communist beliefs no more relevant to his possible employment than the color of his skin. Hutchins did not go into the relative validity of Communists beliefs as against skin color as an index to probable future behavior, this being a question of fact and therefore outside the scope of the curiously disembodied kind of logic he applies to the world.

Not that this quality isn't sometimes an advantage for one who would defend civil liberties today.

"Dr. Hutchins, do you think it's good Americanism to take the Fifth?" a reporter asked.

"The Fifth Amendment is part of the Constitution," stoutly replied the Doctor.

A fortnight later, asked on a "Meet the Press" television program whether or not he would hire a Communist, Hutchins hedged slightly, declining to give a yes-or-no answer. "There are many gradations of membership in Communist organizations," he said. This apparently implies that a full-fledged Communist would not be welcome on the Fund's payroll, and may indicate that the Doctor's logic is becoming more corporeal.

Hutchins runs the Fund with his usual Aristotelian dash. "It's just an anti-absurdity project," he says, and proceeds to lay down a number of take-it-or-leave-it propositions, etched in the sharpest black and white, along the lines of "Either you're for civil rights or you're not. If you're for them, then . . ." When a newly hired employee reported for duty at the Fund's offices in the Tuerck mansion, in Pasadena, from which Hutchins directs high policy, the president advised him to begin work by spending a couple of weeks thinking. He shows little interest in details; consulted on some specific problem by a subordinate, he is likely to wave it aside, saying, "That's your baby, not mine." In the same spirit, at last fall's press conference he admitted, with ill-concealed pride, "I'm not an expert on Communism," a reprise of his lofty reply to a 1949 Illinois legislative committee that asked him what he thought of the Communist Party: "I am not instructed on this subject." Several of the Fund's more serious and sympathetic critics think it could achieve its aims better, and maybe even occasionally avoid the kind of damaging "controversies" (read: "hatchet jobs") from which it has suffered, if the Doctor and his staff were a little better instructed on Communism, say up to the high-school level. But in Dr. Hutchins' bright lexicon there is no such word as humility. "I am surprised that there should be any differences of opinion about the Fund for the Republic," he observed last fall, on receiving the Bill of Rights Award of the American Veterans Committee. "They must result from misinformation."

Hutchins' whole career, from one rather jaundiced point of view, can be described as that of a bright young sophomore who becomes a college president without ever ceasing to be a sophomore. The story is told that Abraham Flexner during the twenties was given a special fund by the Rockefeller Foundation to help talented younger men. He is said to have offered Hutchins, who was then the boy-wonder Assistant Dean of the Yale Law School, $10,-000 so he could take a couple of years off to read, reflect, and generally deepen his wisdom. Hutchins turned down the offer, shortly afterward became Dean, and a few years later President of the University of Chicago. Running into Flexner at some academic function, Hutchins said, "If I'd taken your ten thousand, I wouldn't be President of the University." "Maybe not," replied Flexner, "but you would have been prepared to be." At the Fund for the Republic, Hutchins has been showing the same traits he did at Chicago and as an associate director of the Ford Foundation—great verve and courage in pushing unorthodox and in general sensible ideas, combined with superficiality, arrogance, poor judgment about people, and a congenital lack of maturity both in understanding specific situations and in effectively dealing with them. In short, the classic sophomore type, with all his vivid potentialities and his muted actualities—but a sixty-year-old sophomore.

The Fund for the Republic's operating headquarters is in New York. A sleekly modern suite on the top floor of a skyscraper on Forty-second Street, just off Madison Avenue, it is in charge of the Fund's vice-president, W. H. Ferry, the genial son of a Detroit automobile magnate. Mr. Ferry, or Ping, as he is known to old friends of at least thirty minutes' standing, displays on the wall of his office a sampler with the flower-embroidered motto "Feel Free," and this legend is also inscribed on match books lying around the place. He obviously feels free himself, and wants his callers, who can reach him directly on the phone without any intervening secretary, to feel free, too. He even wants the New York Public Library to feel free; the Fund has given it $2,000 for no better, and no worse, reason than that "we use it a lot." Ferry has been described by Hutchins as "the kind of man I need for the job—interesting and interested," and by Fulton Lewis, Jr., as "a constant dissenter on almost everything and a rebel against everything conventional." Mr. Lewis has also complained that "the record of Ping Ferry is a continuous story of extreme radicalism on the crusading level," apparently referring to Ferry's nine months, years ago, as public-relations director of the C.I.O. Political Action Committee. The rest of "the record" consists of one year teaching Latin and coaching football at the Choate School, several years as a cub reporter in Detroit, and a much longer term with Earl Newsom & Co., which handles public relations for Ford Motors. In short, Ferry's past experience in Left Wing politics and civil liberties has been even more limited than that of his chief. If good intentions, courage, and logic, untrammelled by very much knowledge of the chancy field they work in, are sufficient, then the Messrs. Hutchins and Ferry will make good use of the Fund's $15,000,000.

The Behavioral Sciences

The Ford Foundation's Behavioral Sciences Program is headed by Dr. Bernard Berelson, a brisk young sociologist from the University of Chicago. Dealing with what President Gaither calls the "soft" sciences, as opposed to the "hard" ones, like physics, chemistry, and biology, the Program's spending has been small compared to the total Foundation budget—a mere $8,000,000 up to the end of 1954. However, the Ford Foundation has gone far beyond Carnegie and Rockefeller in its enthusiasm for the soft sciences, and in 1955 it stepped up its spending with the announcement of a $15,000,000 program in mental-health research. The behavioral sciences were Gaither's special province during his first years with the Foundation. At that time, he summarized their unsatisfactory state:

If you examine the field carefully, you quickly discover a startling disorder. Many of these subjects, though they call themselves sciences, lack the important characteristics of science. . . . A natural science like physics consists of experiment, the accumulation of data, the framing of general theories, attempts to verify the theories, and prediction. . . .

There is very little of this here. Experiment is, of course, difficult. But for the most part these sciences are content with the accumulation of data. Theories are framed but rarely verified, for there is no universal standard for the verification process. And what theories there are seem to be either particular theories, designed to cover the accumulated data and no more, or theories so general they are useless for prediction, like "the law of supply and demand." There is also a disturbing discontinuity. Although the various branches of the field should be capable of reinforcing and stimulating each other, they work in isolation.

There are those who say that the behavioral sciences are soft because that is their nature, and that attempts to harden them by imitating the quantitative, measuring, verifying approach of physics and chemistry lead merely to grandiose and sterile "group projects," since the amount of data required is more than one person can gather or handle. The results of the projects, it is further claimed, are neither scientific (since the units measured are too disparate and the factors involved too variable, complex, intangible, and subtle to permit hard answers) nor creative, like the work of such great, and soft, pioneers as Hobbes, Rousseau, Bentham, Marx, Veblen, Mill, de Tocqueville, Weber, and Freud. Although Dr. Berelson has expressed misgivings (as well as satisfaction) about the dominance today of the hard approach, his division appears, on the whole, to favor it, which means it also favors group projects. Nor is it alone in taking this tack; a chart in *Fortune* for November, 1955, shows that the percentage of research papers written by two or more authors appearing in the leading economic, sociological, psychological, and political journals has increased greatly since 1920. Dr. Berelson was puzzled to observe that William H. Whyte, Jr., the author of the accompanying article, which criticized the foundations for neglecting the individual scholar, had presented the chart as a Horrible Example. "Why, it might even show we're getting more scientific!" he exclaimed.

Dr. Berelson's Program has, to be sure, paid some atten-

tion to the individual; it has paid out $150,000 for fellow-
ships to graduate students who had not previously been
majoring in any behavioral science (these are called "seduc-
tion fellowships" in the trade) and, more importantly,
$297,000, in grants of $5,500 each, to fifty-four behavioral
scientists. These grants, which were made in 1952, were
"free"—that is, the recipients could use them as they liked,
without having to work up a "project"—and they were so
successful (according to Whyte, "the scholars husbanded
the money with care; they spent it on vital, not 'busy,'
work; and they explored ideas that might otherwise have
atrophied") that the Foundation recently appropriated
$425,000 for a new series of free grants to individuals. But
the great bulk of the spending has been for group projects,
such as $1,400,000 to the University of Chicago Law
School for "an extensive research program on law and the
behavioral sciences"; $185,000 divided among six groups of
scholars who are making "propositional inventories" in political behavior, social stratification, child development, organization theory, economic development and cultural
change, and communications (Dr. Berelson says that these
inventories aspire to summarize all the "proved generalizations" that can be made in each field on the basis of
present knowledge and then to arrange the generalizations
in logical order as a series of propositions, an undertaking that has a grandeur worthy even of the Ford Foundation); $200,000 to Drs. Eleanor and Sheldon Glueck, of
Harvard, to supervise research into juvenile delinquency;
$600,000 for something rather unhappily described as "re-
search and training in population growth," to be conducted
by the Population Council, which was established in 1952
by a gift from John D. Rockefeller III; and $875,000 to
the Center for International Studies, at Massachusetts Institute of Technology, for a big group project devoted to
"élite international communications." (In this case, "communications" means not cables but all the means by which

people's minds are influenced, from movies and newspapers to back-yard gossip, while "élite" refers not to the four hundred but to "the opinion leaders" and "the decision makers.")

Betwixt and between group and individual is a grant of $3,500,000 to build and maintain for five years the Center for Advanced Study in the Behavioral Sciences, at Palo Alto, California. The Center, which was opened in the fall of 1954, is housed in elegantly modern buildings; an article describing it and entitled "A Humane Campus for the Study of Man," in a recent issue of *Architectural Forum*, rhapsodizes: "There is a warmth of redwood, a material sure of touching automatically the emotional antennae of man; there is also the more intense mental approach to modern interiors . . . to discipline and direct the exuberance of the wood." In this highly charged architectural setting, a group of thirty-eight behavioral scientists, chosen from among some three thousand candidates, spent the 1954–55 academic year, at their usual salaries, working and studying, alone or together, as they chose. About half of these fellows, as they are called, were well-established authorities—men like Clyde Kluckhohn, of Harvard, Harold Lasswell, of Yale, and Paul Lazarsfeld, of Columbia. The others, younger, were, or were believed to be by the selecting committee, men of promise. The behavioral problem of organizing life at the Center soon arose—planning vs. laissez faire, freedom vs. organization. "They often wished Ralph [Dr. Ralph Tyler, the director] would structure it," explains Dr. Berelson. "But he remained permissive." The problem was finally worked out by the fellows themselves, who set up small groups, each of which met regularly to discuss some special subject. It was soon found necessary to limit attendance at these meetings to the regular members. "Some outsider would keep corrupting the discussion," one observer has reported. "Those with a core interest, as against a merely peripheral one, found they could not develop their vocabularies."

A behavioral scientist with an undeveloped vocabulary is a fish out of water, a turtle on its back. There is little danger, however, that the vocabularies of practitioners in the field will not be adequately developed. The Ford Foundation is taking care of that. A typical Ford project is a $174,000 "cross-cultural" (different tribes or countries) study of child development that teams at Yale, Harvard, and Cornell are now making; team members are given a basic manual entitled *Field Guide for a Study of Socialization in Five Societies,* which contains, among other things, full instructions on how to make "a funnel-type open-ended interview with probes," which sounds like a plumber's tool but isn't. "Funnel-type" means that the interviewer directs all his questions toward one point, "open-ended" means that the questions are so worded that the respondent can answer more than "Yes" or "No," and "probes" are stimulating interjections by the interviewer, which may be either "non-directive" ("That's interesting" or "Uh-huh") or "directive" ("But don't you think . . . ?" or "Nonsense!"). The *Guide* also contains a rather thorough definition of "succorance," which should be of interest to parents: "Refers to tendencies to await the nurturant response of another, accept the nurturant response of another, or signal to another the wish for nurturance. . . . Succorant behavior . . . consists of crying and thrashing about, and later in infancy any other vocalizations or motor responses which appear to develop as signals to caretakers." That would about seem to cover it.

Resources for the Future

The $10,000,000 appropriated since 1950 by the Ford Foundation for economic development and administration has practically all been spent during the Gaither regime. Almost half has gone to Resources for the Future, Inc., an autonomous fund the Foundation set up in 1952, with headquarters in Washington. Its president is Reuben G. Gustavson, formerly Chancellor of the University of Nebraska. A big, rugged, slow-spoken man, Gustavson, unlike some others who have been connected with the Foundation, believes in proceeding deliberately. "We've got seven hundred thousand dollars a year for the next five years," he says. "That's enough for us now. We want to feel our way." (That spending $700,000 a year is "feeling our way" will appear odd only to those unaccustomed to the Ford scale of philanthropy.) Resources for the Future deals with "the current position and future outlook" of every kind of natural resource, from land, oil, coal, and electricity to fish, cows, and trees, and it approaches its subject from every angle, including regional planning, the non-military use of atomic energy, and "economic and social development in smaller watersheds." Among its directors are Stanley Ruttenberg, education and research director of the C.I.O.; William S. Paley, chairman of the Columbia Broadcasting System; Horace M. Albright, president of the United States Potash Company; and the ubiquitous Beardsley Ruml.

The rest of the $10,000,000 allotted to economic studies has gone mainly for a seven-year investigation of economics and politics in India, Indonesia, and Italy that is being made by the Center for International Studies at M.I.T. ($1,050,000); to a group of economists who are analyzing "labor as a factor in economic development" ($475,000); to the University of Pennsylvania for a series of studies on consumer behavior ($500,000); and to the Brookings Institution to support its researches in American economy and government ($1,000,000).

Perspectives USA

Although the Ford Foundation, unlike Carnegie and Rockefeller, has shown no interest in the arts and the humanities as such, it runs two cultural enterprises of its own—its quarterly *Perspectives USA* and a television show called "Omnibus."

Perspectives USA is published by Intercultural Publications, Inc.—one of those independent dependencies the Foundation goes in for—which is headed by James Laughlin, the founder and owner of the offbeat publishing house, New Directions. *Perspectives USA* is a sort of literary appendix to the Foundation's international program and comes under its budget. The aim of the quarterly is "to give readers abroad a representative picture of the intellectual and artistic life of the United States." (Intercultural imports as well as exports culture, getting together special supplements of contemporary foreign writing which have been published, in English, in the *Atlantic Monthly*. It drops $150,000 a year on this operation.) *Perspectives USA* resembles *Partisan Review, Kenyon Review, Sewanee Review, Hudson Review, Accent,* and other "little" magazines in its content, and, in fact, a good deal of it is reprinted from them, but it differs in having a very plush format, with color plates, and in costing $170,000 a year to put out, which is more than all the others together spend. It prints editions in four languages—English, French, German, and Italian—with a total of around 40,000 copies, which it sells in sixty countries. In this country, where it doesn't care much about circulation, *Perspectives USA* sells for a dollar and a half a copy, which is above cost, but abroad it goes for from thirty-five to fifty cents, which is way below. Its biggest sale is in Germany (12,000 copies), followed by Italy (7,000), England (4,000), and France (3,000). Although *Perspectives USA* has played it safe, sticking to the well-established names in the literary canon, and lately modulating from the academic avant-garde to the academic academic (a typical early title was "Technique as Joy— Observations on the Poetry of E. E. Cummings"; a typical latter-day one is "The American Organizational Economy"), and although Mr. Laughlin, having become alarmed, like other foundation people, by the Congressional investigations of foundations in the past four years, has tended to exclude material critical of the American Way of Life, there is no evidence that the Foundation's trustees have become infatuated with *Perspectives USA*—or, for opposite reasons, that many American intellectuals have. The effect it gives, compared to other "little" magazines, is of a richly dressed drum major who has somehow wound up at the end of the parade. The venture has been criticized, on practical grounds, as needlessly expensive and as likely to antagonize literary circles abroad by competing at cut rates with their own struggling magazines. Someone suggested a while ago that *Perspectives USA* could accomplish its aim more cheaply and with less friction if it simply subsidized the translation and placing of American articles in foreign magazines. This modest proposal has lately been adopted and put into effect. The magazine, however, will continue to be published by Intercultural Publications until the fall of 1956, when a recent $500,000 "terminal grant" from the Foundation will terminate.

"Omnibus"

The Foundation's television show is an hour-and-a-half miscellany called "Omnibus," which for the last three years has gone out over the C.B.S. network on Sunday afternoons. Its purpose, according to Robert Saudek, its producer, who came to the job after nine years as a radio-and-television executive, is "to attract a mass audience large enough to interest commercial sponsors in pro-

grams which contain values of information and enlighten-
ment calculated to help raise not only television's program
standards but also the general level of American taste and
interests." The objective of attracting a mass audience and
interesting commercial sponsors has been achieved; the
show is regularly watched by around 17,000,000 people,
as near as such statistics can be figured, and in the 1954–55
season it almost broke even on its annual budget of $1,500,-
000 (although up to the middle of the 1955–56 season it
was shy two sponsors and so was losing money). But its
success in raising program standards and the level of public
taste is debatable. "We were determined not to be pious,
sanctimonious, holier-than-thou," says Mr. Saudek in re-
calling the mood in which "Omnibus" was started. "We
took people at their own value. We knew they didn't want
to be uplifted but to be entertained intelligently." The
keynote of a brochure that was put out to attract sponsors
—or, as the "Omnibus" people delicately call them, "sub-
scribers"—in advance of the show's début was constant
reassurance that it wouldn't be too intellectual: " 'Omnibus'
will be aimed straight at the average American audience
. . . neither highbrow nor lowbrow . . . but the audience
that made the great circulations of such magazines as
Reader's Digest, Life, the *Ladies' Home Journal* . . . the
audience which is the solid backbone of any business, as
it is of America itself."

For its master of ceremonies, "Omnibus" selected
Alistair Cooke, the American correspondent of the Man-
chester *Guardian.* It was an inspired choice. Mr. Cooke is
a kind of cultural headwaiter who simultaneously intimi-
dates and flatters the customers, being impeccably dressed
(but in a casual way), fluently articulate (but easy to
follow), British as to accent (but American in the easy
bonhomie of his manner—"My name, by the way, is
Alistair Cooke"). The brochure presented Mr. Cooke as a
mental heavyweight ("perhaps the century's foremost in-

terpreter of America") with a style guaranteed not to
extend the lightest-weight brain in his audience ("He will
be the Good Companion always welcome in your home
for his fresh and witty slant . . . the kind of fellow you
will be glad to have drop in every Sunday afternoon,
because he always leaves you with a new story to tell, a
new subject to talk about, a new sense of expanded hori-
zons").

Among the features making up "three representative
programs" listed in the brochure were "A Yankee Looks
at a Cricket Match—well-known comedian describes in his
own befuddled way what he thinks is going on," "Alone
with Harpo Marx," "The Jungle of Dr. Schweitzer,"
"Plastics, the Alchemy of Today—Editorial Feature about
the industry represented by one of the sponsors," and
"Renaissance Man: a Portrait from *Life*'s History of Western Man—conducted and narrated by Leopold Stokowski."
Although none of these particular features materialized, the
actual broadcasts have also combined the sublime and the
ridiculous, the serious and the meretricious, in the kind
of mélange that our middle-brow cultural entrepreneurs
have found to be commercially profitable. At one time or
another, "Omnibus" has come up with Beethoven and a
visit to a retired race horse; *King Lear* (with Orson
Welles) and the world's champion figure-skater; Jack
Benny and Chekhov; Coach Lou Little, of Columbia, explaining football plays and a Gertrude Stein playlet. Some
of the weekly passengers on "Omnibus" have been un-
deniably distinguished—for example, a fine presentation of
Sophocles' *Antigone,* in the Fitts-Fitzgerald translation;
"Toby and the Tall Corn," a lively and charming docu-
mentary about a Middle Western tent show, got up by
Russell Lynes; a sensitive dramatic adaptation of Pamela
Frankau's "The Duchess and the Smugs," made by Ellen
Violett, with Susan Strasberg in the lead; and Leonard

Bernstein's "The World of Jazz." But the great majority of the passengers on "Omnibus" have been run-of-the-mill.

The show also has a disturbing habit of falling flat on its face when it tries to soar. One instance was the recent hour and a half of hopped-up travelogue about the Renaissance, which was not meretricious in the way the *Life*-Stokowski treatment projected by the brochure would have been, but which managed to fail in its own way. The role of Burton Holmes was divided between Mr. Cooke, operating in his suavest this-won't-hurt-a-bit manner ("Now, 'renaissance' is a French word meaning rebirth"), and the movie actor Charlton Heston, all dressed up like a cinquecento Davy Crockett. An earlier example was an hour-and-half version of *The Iliad*, which was painlessly (or painfully, depending on the point of view) m.c.'d by Mr. Cooke ("The story is about a buccaneer named Paris who went cruising in the Aegean Sea") and which presented a subdeb Helen and a petulant Achilles struggling with un-Homeric passages such as the latter's speech early in the drama: "Ajax, you're welcome. Odysseus, welcome. No, you're more than welcome. Patroclus, big cups for great rascals. It's time you came to see me. Patroclus here, he's dull company. Full of arguments. I'm glad, I'm glad you came." The show was written by Andrew K. Lewis, who is on the staff of "Omnibus" and who spent a solid year on the job, rewriting the script five times. Out of all this effort came the replacing of Homer's lines (which really aren't at all bad) with lines like the above. Also: " 'I'm sorry for that man Hector,' said Zeus." And yet again: "You don't know how it is to be a woman. I had a husband. And when he was gone, just like your wife, I waited. . . . No, you don't care. It's a long time now, I'm old."

"Omnibus" has certainly avoided becoming highbrow—the British Broadcasting Company's Third Programme need not look to its laurels—but there is some disagreement as to what else it has accomplished as a form of entertainment. The *Herald Tribune* has editorially saluted the show as "unfalteringly dedicated to the principle that television can operate successfully on the adult level," and last year "Omnibus" won a Peabody Award. An opposite point of view has been expressed by Jack Gould, the *Times* television critic, who has elegized its decline and fall: "Once the Foundation may have had some claim to the role of a pioneer in TV productions; today, regular commercial television often runs rings around the ["Omnibus"] workshop in cultural accomplishment. . . . The Ford Foundation is pursuing the one goal that, more than any other, has accounted for mediocrity in the broadcasting arts . . . trying to please as many people as possible at one time. 'Omnibus,' in short, is acutely rating-conscious; it fires cultural buckshot. . . . 'Omnibus' has grown notorious for its pliant susceptibility to commercial promotional gimmicks."

Apropos of Mr. Gould's last remark, there is the experience of the housing expert Charles Abrams, now chairman of the New York State Commission Against Discrimination, who was invited to discuss housing problems on the show—such, at least, was his impression. On arriving at the "Omnibus" office, he was handed a script that roughed out for him the role of straight man to some rhetorical questions. After a few introductory questions about the seriousness of the housing problem throughout the world, the gist of the next one was, "Mr. Abrams, don't you think that prefabrication is one answer to the housing crisis in Latin America and other underdeveloped areas?" "Yes" was to be his reply. The script then called for Mr. Abrams to be guided into a prefabricated aluminum house made by an "Omnibus" sponsor, Aluminium, Ltd., of Canada, and to say, "Very interesting, indeed." Since he had just returned from a United Nations mission to the Gold Coast, where a political crisis had been caused by the government's policy of importing expensive prefabricated units instead of using the much cheaper native labor and materials, Mr. Abrams asked whether he could change the script to make it conform with his opinion. He was told he couldn't, because it was a commercial. Mr. Abrams thereupon left, suggesting on his way out that they would be fairer to their audience if they hired a paid performer like Fred Allen.

Mr. Saudek, on the other hand, states that he has rejected "a number of advertisers who sought to place some program condition on their purchase." He also states that George Benson, the only member of his staff who has any contact with sponsors, "has nothing to do with editorial policy," but since it was precisely Mr. Benson who conducted the abortive negotiations with Mr. Abrams over a commercial that did its best to impersonate editorial matter, this leads to the on-the-other-*other*-hand conclusion that the hands of Esau don't synchronize with the voice of Jacob any more than they used to. It is a complicated world.

Nor does the world—the "Omnibus" sector of it, that is —become less complex when one considers the theory behind the show's commercials. In its advance brochure, "Omnibus" offered each of its five potential sponsors the chance to produce "a unique five-minute commercial, based on your business, every fifth week," the uniqueness lying in the fact that it was to be not just another commercial but something that would stand up as an educational feature, with the sponsor's product as the theme. ("'Omnibus' encouraged its sponsors to create commercials that would blend into its program format and make friends for themselves and for 'Omnibus,'" noted the trade journal *Printers' Ink*, in its issue of July 3, 1953.) Praiseworthy as this appears from one point of view—as an attempt to civilize the barbarous commercial—from another, it is a still further blurring of the increasingly tenuous boundary between commercials and entertainment in TV, a "fuzzing-it-up" process that goes beyond anything the ordinary, or non-philanthropic, programs have yet ventured. From this standpoint, using the authority of an expert to tout the sponsor's product, as was attempted with Mr. Abrams, is a less straightforward approach than simply paying an actor to do the job. The moral ambiguities reach a crescendo when Mr. Benson, after insisting that the script he showed Abrams was plainly identified as a commercial, adds, "If an expert shared the viewpoint expressed in the advertising, he would have been paid," which stimulates reflections on the courtroom use of experts as witnesses for one or the other interested party, not to mention those white-jacketed doctors in the cigarette ads. As of the 1955–56 season, "Omnibus" has retreated from its "unique five-minute commercials" to the plain garden variety, possibly recognizing that it had been skating on thinner ice than it had realized.

From the beginning, "Omnibus" seems to have put attracting sponsors first and raising the level of television second; the Foundation's trustees originally expressed the "hope" that the show would become self-supporting within two or three years—and a trustee's hope is not a fragile thing. When a children's television program called "Excursion," another Foundation venture, failed to break even in its first season, it was dropped, despite excellent notices and an enthusiastic response from parents. It could be, however, that the trouble with "Omnibus" lies deeper than the Ford trustees' dollar-mindedness—in an overfondness for "names," a lack of originality (not long ago, the program's 17,000,000 viewers were taken Behind the Scenes at Grand Central Terminal to see How a Great Railroad Is Run, a theme that might have interested the editors of *St. Nicholas* magazine back in the nineties), an exaggerated fear of boring an audience whose capacity it may well underestimate. Mr. Saudek seems honestly convinced he is bringing culture—or a reasonable facsimile thereof—to the masses, and thinks criticism of "Omnibus" must proceed from intellectual snobbishness. The shoe may be on the other foot, however. There may be a much bigger audience for first-rate TV material than the super-democratic drivers of "Omnibus" realize. In an effort to avoid snobbery, one may fall into condescension.

CHAPTER 5

THE PHILANTHROPOIDS

THE FORD FOUNDATION offices at 477 Madison Avenue were designed by the firm of Skidmore, Owings & Merrill, which did Lever House, and are in the most discreetly expensive modern style. Chastity is carried to the point of antisepsis, with gray and beige the dominant colors. All the offices, and even the corridors, are carpeted—an arrangement that is at once sumptuous and democratic, and thus a true expression of the Foundation's personality. (It is also painful, for the carpet causes every door handle to administer a slight, waspish shock of static electricity.) Some members of the staff feel that this elegance is not appropriate to a foundation that deals with scholars, scientists, and other persons of modest income, and would prefer a more rundown setting in a less glittering quarter of the city, or even in some outlying college town. But the Ford Foundation is a $2,500,000,000 proposition, and it is hard for so much money not to dress the part.

The crucial decisions in the Foundation's work—namely, who or what will get slices of the tens, and latterly hundreds of millions it gives away—are made by a group of about fifty people, consisting of its fourteen trustees and some forty philanthropoids. A philanthropoid—the term

95

large foundations not only issue regular reports but   also submit willingly to journalistic inquiries into their work-ings. The Ford Foundation has a conscientious Office of Reports, the sole function of which is providing informa-tion to whoever wants it. The Office is headed by Porter McKeever, who is youngish, earnest, sincere, unpreten-tious, and friendly, and whose previous jobs have included serving as chief press officer of the American delegation to the United Nations and as publicity director of Citizens for Stevenson during the 1952 campaign. Mr. McKeever's —or, rather, Porter's—office takes its title seriously enough to have distributed 60,000 copies of the 1954 Annual Report.

The usual philanthropoidal background is academic, but at Ford the prevailing type is more likely to have been connected with the government or with one of the com-mittees, commissions, councils, agencies, associations, so-cieties, institutes, boards, and bureaus without which Americans seem unable to do anything except make money. Some representative former jobs of Ford, philanthropoids are program director of the Committee for the Interna-tional Trade Organization, chief of the Division of Inter-national Security Affairs of the State Department's Bureau of United Nations' Affairs, president of the Alaska Rural Rehabilitation Corporation, director of the Chicago Coun-cil on Foreign Relations, research director of the Bureau of Applied Social Research at Columbia University, direc-tor of the Labor Office of the Office of Price Administra-tion, and field director of the Division of Program Surveys in the Bureau of Agricultural Economics of the United States Department of Agriculture. As this sort of back-ground might suggest, and as Mr. Westbrook Pegler gloom-ily suspects, the Ford philanthropoid is of a liberal turn politically, habituated to collective, nonprofit enterprise, and inclined more toward internationalism than isolation-ism. He appears to be serious, even idealistic, about his work, and he gives every evidence of enjoying it; the cynicism prevalent elsewhere on Madison Avenue has not infected the Ford Foundation. And, indeed, his work combines the moral glow of a Worthy Cause with a salary that is comfortable, if not luxurious. A hundred dollars is about the same in his personal life as a million is to him professionally; when he has lunch—at Schrafft's—with colleagues from other foundations, he is used to such kidding as, "Have you spent your million for today yet?" His living standards perk up when he travels on an expense account, and thus comes more directly into the Foundation's well-heeled orbit; so do those of his grantees and consultants, who sometimes feel guilty about being permitted, and even encouraged, to take taxis, engage clerical help, and otherwise spend "as much as you need to do a good job." One professor who was brought to New York for a week by the Foundation and established in the Hotel Pierre found it impossible to overcome his ingrained habits of thrift. "I'll bet I'm the only man in town who's living at the Pierre and eating at Nedick's," he remarked to a friend.

The philanthropoids at Ford communicate with each other in a special jargon, the lingua franca of the foundation world; it is a scholarly jive, with traces of the argot of the surrounding Madison Avenue account-executive region, and it might be called philanthropese. At times, its purpose is to relax and reassure, to make it clear that the speaker is not on a higher intellectual level than the most modestly endowed of his audience—as, indeed, he usually is not. "Now, I'm not quite sure how the discussion ought to roll," the chairman of a round table may begin, and, in fact, *has* begun. "But let's just bat it around a little and see where the ball comes out. No holds barred and we *do* want to have a real meeting of minds." At other times, quite to the contrary, it is a professional shorthand, com-

prehensible only to fellow-initiates. When a Ford philanthropoid defines the ideal project as one that (a) is self-
liquidating, (b) has plenty of leverage, and is both (c)
programmed from within and (d) a response to a felt
need, he means (a) that it will either be completed or taken
over by someone else after a reasonable period, (b) that it
stimulates others to put in money, too, (c) that the members of the staff didn't merely open their mail but thought
up the project themselves, and (d) that it is something the
beneficiaries feel they need, as opposed to something they
just passively accept.

Although philanthropoidal life at Ford is more sober
than sparkling, with no office characters or jokes—"Perhaps we're a little too serious around here," one staff member has admitted—and although about the only incident
approaching drama that has recently occurred in those
antiseptic quarters was the theft, over a weekend, of $1,700
cash from the office safe, and even that was definitely not
an inside job, philanthropese is a lively language—perhaps
to make up for the sobriety of the professional matters
for which it is used. Some key terms are "grass roots";
"perspective" ("He's been away long enough to get some
perspective on it"); "pinpoint" ("I want to pinpoint the
factor of variability in these estimates"—a sentence in
which either "highlight" or "showcase" may be substituted
for "pinpoint," all three expressions being examples of a
tendency in modern foundation jargon to use nouns as
verbs in an effort to achieve forcefulness, however spuri-
ous); "grass roots"; "think through" ("I wonder if Don
has really thought through the implications of his proposal"); "tailor" ("The program is tailored to the felt
needs of the community"); "built-in" ("Can we keep an
eye on progress through some built-in evaluation procedures?"); "topflight" ("a well-rounded group of topflight
men in the field"—cf. "I'm flying low today," meaning
"I'm not feeling very well today"); "grass roots"; "brief"

("We're briefing him on local conditions"); "challenge" (this word, as in "What confronts us here is a stimulating challenge to us all," has a peculiar attraction, or challenge, for philanthropoids, to whom life is real, earnest, and full of problems); "germinal" ("A small grant might have germinal possibilities," from which it follows that a terminal grant is a germinal grant gone to seed); "maximize" ("We'll bring together some topflighters and maximize their experience"); "rundown," "button up," "kick off" ("Let's give the project a final rundown tomorrow, button it up Friday, and kick off the field survey next week"); "carbon" (used as a verb, as, "I'll carbon you in" for "I'll see that you get a copy"); "grass roots"; "spearhead" ("a subcommittee to spearhead the attack on the problem"); "bird-dog" ("I can't find that evaluation report, Jack. Will you bird-dog it for me in the files?"); "to get mileage out of" (to make use of, as "The Nobel people certainly get a lot of mileage, publicity-wise, out of their $200,000 a year!"); "frame of reference"; "develop a clearer picture"; and, of course, "grass roots," which is an interesting example of the attempt to compensate in language for what is felt to be lacking in reality.

Philanthropese is the esoteric language, for use among philanthropoids in their inter-office memoranda and in the staff and committee meetings at which they spend a great deal of their time. (When a philanthropoid's secretary says he is in conference, she generally means it, poor fellow.) There is also an exoteric language, which might be called foundationese, for communication with the outside world, which is developed most fully in the Annual Report, a literary product that is somewhat more readable than the phone book and somewhat less so than the collected sermons of Henry Ward Beecher. This language is, like Latin, a dead language, written rather than spoken, and designed for ceremony rather than utility. Its function is magical and incantatory—not to give information or to communicate

its problems. He subsidizes research on everything he or some ingenious grantee can think of, such as the $50,000 apiece Ford gave to five universities for "self-studies" of their work in the behavioral sciences, which produced five thick volumes (Harvard's ran to 518 pages) whose most important practical conclusion was that what is chiefly needed is more grants ("practical" is putting it mildly; recently the Foundation divided $1,350,000 among four of the five introspective behavioral-science departments, a sum which will now be used to produce more research); or the total of $475,000 it gave to four universities for an "analysis of the labor factor in economic development," the first of whose "specific objectives" was "to develop the knowledge for a generalized concept of the labor factor in the modern world"; or the $100,000 it turned over to the Carnegie Endowment for International Peace—a foundation which, of sad necessity, specializes in the production of voluminous reports that it hopes will be read by somebody somewhere who can Do Something About It—to help finance "a two-year program of studies of national policies and attitudes toward the United Nations," which is like making a map of a cloud hovering over a fog. If nothing else occurs to the philanthropoid, he will commission a survey of his own activities. This is called a self-evaluation, and it can achieve such proportions as a two-hundred-page report on the Foundation's Foreign Area Fellowship Program, whose diligent author, among other labors, interviewed a hundred and sixty people. It was an intelligent report, but one wonders whether, at times, the native hue of action may not be sicklied o'er with the pale cast of evaluation.

This is by no means a problem unique to the Ford Foundation. About five years ago, one of the leading "little" literary magazines needed money desperately if it was to survive. The editors got in touch with the Rockefeller Foundation and were cordially invited in for an interview. The philanthropoid-in-charge listened most sympathetically to their plea for help, and then told them that the Foundation was indeed concerned about the survival of magazines such as theirs, so vital to the survival of democratic culture, and had, in fact, decided to do something about it. So it was undertaking a survey. (A philanthropoid would deal with the problem of a man trapped in a burning house by subsidizing a study of combustion.) Four years later, the Rockefeller Foundation came through with a modest grant to the magazine in question, which had managed to pull through somehow. But the Foundation is still pondering the general problem of little-magazine economics, in much the same spirit as the Lady Bountiful who worries about the deserving poor (the undeserving, as is well known, use bathtubs exclusively for the storage of coal). "Do you think it would make them [the little magazines] soft," President Rusk once asked a visitor, "if they knew where their next subsidy was coming from?" The visitor said he didn't. Dean Rusk looked thoughtful.

A bit of philanthropoidal research that is especially interesting, because it is so typically uninteresting, is the "evaluation of experience of foreign students who are studying or have studied in the United States" that the Social Science Research Council carried on from 1952 to 1955 with $225,-000 in funds provided by the Big Three—Ford, Rockefeller, and Carnegie. "The general purpose," stated a preliminary report, "is to develop techniques for evaluating the impact of exchange-of-persons experiences on foreign students in order to produce, through intensive controlled investigation, a body of information on the effect of exchange that can serve as a basis for a wider analysis of the many variable factors in particular exchanges [Translation: The Council is spending $225,000 on a study that will make it possible to spend more $$$ on more studies]." The March, 1954, issue of the Council's house organ, *Items*, shed further light: "The first phase had consisted of intensive exploratory studies of the adjustment of foreign students to life on American campuses. . . . As was hoped [Translation: We were disappointed], these studies focussed the attention of the committee on a number of problems of salient theoretical and practical interest, and resulted in the formulation of many hypotheses about the determinants of various outcomes of the students' sojourn. As is generally the case with intensive studies, however, the data served to document varieties of cross-cultural experience rather than to support firm conclusions about causes and effects [Translation: We didn't find out anything]. The committee early decided, therefore, that the next phase of its work would be devoted to well-focussed, systematic studies designed to test hypotheses and attack major problems discerned in the initial phase of its research [Translation: We're starting the whole thing all over]."

This second phase produced a foot-high stack of mimeographed reports that are certainly systematic, although the focus may be a little blurred. Thus, Chapter I of the "Preliminary Report of the Mexican Student Project" begins:

The setting of the Mexican student study is in Southern California, a fairly defined geographic entity comprising the counties of Santa Barbara, Ventura, Los Angeles, Orange, San Diego, San Bernardino, Riverside, Imperial, and, by some reckoning, Kern. The major part of the area . . . is a series of coastal plains and broad basinlike valleys . . . ranging in elevation from sea level to 2500 feet. . . . The higher mountains may be snow-covered several months of the year. . . .

This seems bizarre, even for a first draft not intended for publication. Perhaps it should be added that the committee, in its systematic attack on major problems, left no stone unturned, including coöperation with the Committee on International Exchange of Persons of the Conference Board of Associated Research Councils. The American academic world, thanks partly to the foundations, is becoming a place where committees accumulate and thought decays.

An inevitable, and depressing, question is: What is the

practical effect of the towering mass of research that Ford and the other foundations have erected with their millions? Does anybody read their findings—*can* anybody read them? And if somebody does, what can he do about it? What has been the practical effect of, for example, the series of "Monitoring Studies" of TV programs that the National Association of Educational Broadcasters has made, with dollars provided by the Fund for Adult Education? What results may be expected, and where, from the $1,050,000 that the Ford Foundation has given to date to the Center for International Studies at M.I.T. for a "program of research in economic and political development" in Italy, India, and Indonesia, which consists of forty different studies, the fortieth being nothing less than *The Economic History of Italy, 1860–1950*? "We key the research in the direction of maximum utility," insists a representative of the Center, pointing out that several of its reports have been warmly debated in government circles, and that the sociologists and economists it sends to Italy, India, and Indonesia (which were *not* chosen for study just because they all begin with "I") work closely with government planners in each country and consider it part of their job to give as well as to get information and advice. Nonetheless, a small doubt persists. Will Secretary Dulles, or his opposite numbers of the three "I" countries, or some other actual individuals in positions of power, somehow, someday, find the time and energy to (a) read the $1,050,000 worth of words and (b) translate this expensive and copious information into action? This might seem to be a crass demand. But while the work of a single scholar may sometimes achieve the intellectual, and even aesthetic, interest that a literary or philosophical production has, and so have a legitimate claim to be judged as an end in itself, rather than as merely a means toward some other end, this almost never happens with the products of modern collective research. They are comparable to Standard and Poor's *Cor-*

poration Records, rather than to Kant's *Critique of Pure Reason,* and therefore must be judged by their usefulness alone. The prognosis, on this practical level, does not appear favorable. Americans have a tendency to amass a vast quantity of data on some problem, and then just leave it lay. Indeed, the gathering of data is often a substitute for action.

Commenting on the 1954 Report of the Ford Foundation, the London *Times Literary Supplement,* after saluting it as "an impressive picture of philanthropic activity," continued:

A . . . large sum was devoted to research plans in the field of economics, and in particular to an organization called Resources for the Future, Inc., the purpose of which is "to gather usable facts and to promote broader public interest and understanding so that our natural resources may be wisely utilized." . . . No praise can be too high for the generosity and the enterprise which inform activities of this kind. Should it ever become economically possible to assemble and administer such a fund at home, the pioneer work of the great American charitable institutions will provide a challenging example. Yet a small doubt persists. How far, among such profusion, does the individual plant get lost in gardens so beautifully dug, manured, and weeded? Or more bluntly, what in the world is Resources for the Future, Inc., going to do with all those usable facts?

Or, to cite an even blunter American question about the plethora of foundation-financed research, which appears in *Funds and Foundations,* a recent book by Abraham Flexner, who, at eighty-eight, has a status in the foundation world like that of Bernard Baruch in national politics: "Who reads the books, if written?"

"Why don't you boys just give everybody in the country two bucks apiece and quit?" asked the wife of an executive of the Ford Foundation, looking around at a number of her husband's colleagues at a cocktail party last Christmas. In actual fact, the Ford Foundation, with capital assets of some $2,500,000,000, could give every inhabitant of this country closer to fifteen dollars before it ran out of cash. But if the lady's arithmetic was shaky, her instinct was sound. Giving away money through a foundation is a wearisome and complicated business, vexing to the soul and wearing on the liver. Like an army, the United Nations, and other large bureaucratic organizations, a foundation excretes an extraordinary quantity of words, most of them of stupefying dullness. The proper foundation executive must be able to keep his mind on such passages as the following, all of them drawn from documents that have been produced or perused by the Ford Foundation's executives in the line of duty:

The participants in the program must constantly interrelate the long-range meaning of the findings and their short-term implications. . . .

Each new appointment to the study committee will be made with a view to rounding out and augmenting the knowledge and disciplines which will be brought to bear on the proposed study. . . .

In international affairs the pattern of communication is seldom a one-way reaction to mass media. . . .

For modern man, the prevention of war is not only the most important of problems; it is also the most baffling. . . .

Accordingly, in considering the proposed plan of taxation, the three sets of provisions must be read and interpreted together—the general provisions subparagraph (1) (c) of Article 11, Article 17 and Annex III. . . .

On the other hand, the amended text makes clear that the principle of non-intervention in domestic matters shall not prejudice the power to make non-binding *recommendations* concerning all matters (whether economic, social, cultural or humanitarian) affecting friendly relations among nations or the general welfare of the world's people. . . .

The Foundation's fourteen trustees, prominent and busy men of affairs, are shielded by the staff from the main spate of bureaucratic rhetoric. But they are expected to digest bulky "Program Dockets" containing such roughage as:

A major portion of the funds requested would be used by the two organizations to encourage and assist their constituent groups in expanding and improving their rural improvement programs in underdeveloped areas. This would be done through the organization of regional conferences; the preparation and distribution of pamphlets, newssheets, and other informational material relating to the content and organization of programs; and by providing advice on planning and organizing programs . . . in thousands of individual program centers throughout the world. While the programs of these centers vary a great deal in size and effectiveness, they represent, if only by virtue of their number, a great potential force. Additional assistance that could be provided with the funds requested would enable them to help many of these centers to operate more effectively.

Giving away money, in short, is not as simple as it sounds. "To get angry is an easy matter and in any man's power, or to give away money or to spend it," wrote Aristotle, "but to decide to whom to give it, and how large a sum, and when, and for what purpose, and how is neither in every man's power nor an easy matter. Hence it is that such excellence is rare and praiseworthy and noble." So, too, Thoreau, who wrote, "You must have a genius for charity as well as for anything else. As for doing good, that is one of the professions that are full." Thoreau was definitely not the foundation type, but Aristotle was one of the first philanthropoids. As the tutor of Alexander the Great, he was able to turn his royal pupil's interests toward education and research. Conscientiously, he administered the supporting funds that his patron gave him for his Lyceum and for his ambitious natural-history project, which at one time had a thousand staff members scattered throughout Greece and Asia Minor gathering data. This might be called the first big research team, and if it produced results like the assertion that salamanders are impervious to fire, that scarcely diminishes the parallel. Even Aristotle, however, could hardly have foreseen the special problems that are now involved in the giving away of money through a foundation.

There is, first of all, the problem of *not* giving away money. For every grant made, at least a score of applicants must be turned down. This takes a good deal of time, tact, and nervous energy. ("You just have to get toughened to it," says President Rusk of Rockefeller.) The division between office and personal life is less distinct among philanthropoids than in most other professions. A Ford Foundation executive applying for a visa is likely to be sounded out by the consul, as he stamps the passport, on what the chances are for more Ford spending in his country. Once, at a dinner party, the Gaithers were introduced as the Gaitskills, and they had a fine time until the hostess discovered her error, after which everybody began to talk projects at them. "It's a nice job," the sardonic Robert M. Hutchins used to say when he was an associate director of the Foundation. "You meet so many interested people." Even when advances are made through channels, refusing is a delicate art. There are certain rules for it, based on experience, which the Foundation observes better now than it did in its younger, more innocent days: Never make any specific criticisms of the project for which money is being sought, since this will lead to lengthy argument, in addition to hurting the applicant's feelings; be firm but humble; and, above all, swathe the brute, bare No in ambiguity, compliments, evasions, and referrals to higher authority. Many applicants feel that there is something unsatisfying about dealing with a large institution by letter; people want to See Somebody, to explain to an actual person the true inwardness of their ideas. The former presi-

dent of the Carnegie Corporation, Charles Dollard, dreamed
up the ideal solution: Hire a refugee of distinguished appearance and, if possible, with a spade beard, who speaks
no English, and assign him to the job of sympathetically
listening to applicants who are going to be turned down;
to prepare him for this role, dress him in a cutaway, give
him an impressive title, and install him in a large and imposing office, after first teaching him just two English
sentences, which he will interpolate during pauses—"That
is very interesting" and "I will take it up with my associates."

At Ford, interviewing applicants with unpromising projects is one of the duties of a pleasant man with gentle
brown eyes and a friendly smile who must here be called
Mr. X, since to print his name would be to end, or at
least violently change, his career. Mr. X might be called
Vice-President in Charge of Turndowns. Applicants whose
projects are unpromising but whose connections are important get a fuller treatment, as when Benson Ford recently "sent along" an acquaintance with a hospital project.
The Foundation no longer builds hospitals, and normally
the applicant would have been told—by Mr. X, if he
wanted to See Somebody—that his project was "out of
program," but in this instance the caller was given an hour
with a high Foundation executive. The result, however,
was the same.

The turndown problem was at its most acute in 1951,
the first year of the Foundation's big expansion program,
when little more was generally known about it than that
it had an improbable amount of money to give away. Estimates of the number of applications for grants received
that year run as high as 25,000. Possibly stimulated by the
"bold look" that Hoffman and Hutchins had given the
Foundation, the proposals included a plan for irrigating the
Sahara that would have cost $500,000,000, or exactly what
the newspapers said the Foundation had in its treasury; a

suggestion from a women's peace group that the unforti-
fied American-Canadian border be memorialized as an
example of peaceful coexistence by the planting of a three-
mile-wide strip of flowers along its entire 3,000 miles, at
a cost of $100,000 a mile, which would have left the Foun-
dation $200,000,000 for less urgent projects; and a proposal
to melt the icecap on the South Pole, on the theory that
this would cause the earth to revolve on a neat vertical
axis instead of on the present messy tilted one, and so
would assure the same weather all year round at any given
place on the globe and also tidy up day and night by
making each always a uniform twelve hours.

Now that the Foundation has settled down and the
limits of its program are better known, applications have
dwindled to a trickle of a mere 5,000 a year, of which,
on an average, one in thirty-one hits the jackpot. Their entertainment quality has fallen off, too—"We don't get the
kind we used to get in Pasadena," says Mr. X a little sadly
—but there are still a few moderately bizarre ones. One
woman asked for a grant to support her mother-in-law;
another—for some reason, most of the peculiar requests
come from women—wanted to make "a field study of the
problem of American tourists in Europe" by becoming
one herself; a third offered, cheap, an "antique watch and
chain"; a fourth demanded a scholarship for her son, a "genius in nuclear physics," who turned out to be twelve years
old; and a fifth needed capital to start a boarding house.
Among other projects the Foundation was asked to finance
in 1954 but didn't were a machine to stop hiccuping, the
celebration of the hundredth anniversary of the freeing
of the slaves, and "a product which I call Fizz Drink, the
Atomic Energy Lift, a mental cure strengthening the heart
and muscles and made of Uranium, Bicarbonate of Soda,
and other ingredients." But the great majority of the applications the Foundation turned down in 1954 appear to
have been perfectly sensible if, at times, dull. All sorts of

books were proposed, from a history of the harp to "The Problem of Surplus Value: A Fundamental Analysis of Communism," and all sorts of research projects—on Cornish mines, democracy in Israel, highway-traffic statistics, and so forth. Funds were requested for existing institutions, like the Missouri Historical Society and the Canadian National Ballet, and for help in creating new ones—an agency for scientific news, a secondary school in Nigeria, an experimental hog station in Ecuador. Twenty-eight Boy Scouts wanted to make a good-will trip to Scotland, the Alabama Prison Board needed help in rehabilitating ex-convicts, an editor wanted to start a short-story magazine. Hundreds and hundreds of applicants came forward with plans—for preventing war, for insuring full employment, for simplifying arithmetic, for world disarmament, for racial integration in schools, for a world language, for a new religious order.

Many of these proposals sound not very different from some the Foundation accepted. The difference between success and failure often depends less on the project than on the Ford staff's estimate of the person advancing it. But, whatever the application's merit, or lack of it, the proper philanthropoid never writes "No." He writes: "Thank you for giving me the opportunity to read your most stimulating and interesting proposal for a nationwide five-year survey, to be conducted by a research team of 18,000 graduate students, of the possibility of establishing a string quartet in every school district of the country. It is, indeed, a project. Unfortunately, the Ford Foundation, while fully alive to the unique importance of chamber music in maintaining and extending our democratic culture, does not presently have a program in the fine arts. Furthermore, the $65,000,000 which you estimate would be the annual cost of the survey, while by no means exorbitant, considering that it includes the purchase of 3,500 I.B.M. card-sorting machines per year, would leave us with little or no income for other purposes. It is therefore only fair to tell you quite frankly that our trustees, with whom I am taking up your remarkable proposal at the earliest opportunity, may not feel free to proceed with it at the moment. In the meantime, if you would care to discuss the whole matter with our Mr. X . . ."

Next, there is the problem, once a grant has been made, of how to keep from having to renew it indefinitely. The grantee, naturally enough, doesn't worry about how his grant may affect the foundation making it, since he generally has "a grantee view of the operation," which is philanthropese for "he is only interested in How Much." But to the philanthropoid How Long is at least as important a question. Foundations have occasionally become so barnacled with steady pensioners, who have grown dependent on them for their very existence, that they have lost almost all freedom of maneuver. Some fifteen years ago, the Carnegie Corporation had to scrape its hull clean; it was a painful business. What hardening of the arteries is to the human body, getting loaded up with future commitments is to a foundation. This problem is at its most acute when it comes to dealing with institutional grantees; institutions go on year after year, and if they get a grant one year, they are likely to assume that they will get one the next, and to plan their budgets accordingly. The prudent philanthropoid tries to disabuse them of this illusion. His aim is to get something started that either will be completed or will become self-supporting after a reasonable period of time, thus releasing funds to meet new needs. But unless a grantee is weaned after a certain point, he will never learn to forage for himself. Although this basic fact of foundation life was set forth in the 1949 Study Report in which a committee headed by Gaither outlined a general program for the Ford Foundation, adequate steps were not at first taken to counteract it. At the outset, the Foundation sometimes gave annual grants in such a way that the recipients got the idea that the largess was to be indefinitely renewed, and so undertook expansion programs on the strength of their great expectations. Nowadays, in cases where there is danger of this happening, the Foundation, instead of giving annual grants, gives a lump sum earmarked for a five- or ten-year period and payable in decreasing amounts year by year. Consequently, long before the term is up a chill wind has begun to blow on the necks of the grantees, stimulating them to raise money elsewhere. This avoids last-minute crises and hard feelings.

The classic example of what a foundation can get into if it takes on future commitments too lightly is the pension program of the Carnegie Foundation for the Advancement of Teaching. Andrew Carnegie had become concerned over the economic insecurity of college teachers, and in 1905 he set up the C.F.A.T. to give every professor in the country a free pension. But nobody had thought to make an actuarial study of how much this would cost, and by 1920 it was clear that it would take far more than Carnegie's entire fortune to meet the payments. The roll of pensioners was frozen as of that year, and even so the Carnegie Corporation is currently paying out about $1,000,000 a year to make good on the pre-1917 pension commitments and will continue to make payments through the year 2000. The main burden was shifted, around 1920, to the Teachers Annuity and Insurance Association, supported by the colleges and the teachers as well as by Carnegie funds. That Carnegie and his advisers should have blundered is understandable: it was a pioneer large-scale pension system, the model in many ways for the New Deal and the insurance companies later on; and out of it all did come teachers' pensions, though with more headaches than the sanguine Carnegie expected.

Another thing that came out of it all was the present dominance of the Ph.D. as a *sine qua non* for academic advancement. In handing out pensions to college teachers, the question naturally arose: What *is* a college? (Even Carnegie didn't aspire to, or want to, take care of the myriad "diploma mills" and tiny backwoods religious "colleges.") Henry Pritchett, who was then president of the Carnegie Corporation and who greatly admired the German university system, drew up an "Accepted List" of colleges eligible for Carnegie pensions, one of the most important criteria being that department heads must have Ph.D.'s. This put pressure on colleges to qualify, which put pressure on professors to get Ph.D.'s, which brought about the present Procrustean situation where no amount of scholarly brilliance or teaching flair will make up for the lack of a doctorate. There are those who see in the Ph.D. obsession a major cause of the sterility and mediocrity of our academic life today, and the moral of *that* is: Doing Good is a Complicated Business.

Every foundation has, finally, the problem of bigness, which, naturally, afflicts the Ford Foundation more than it does its colleagues. The Foundation's recent history has been a desperate scramble, like that of Eliza fleeing across the ice floes, to keep ahead of, or at least abreast of, its dizzily mounting income. The 1949 Study Report thought in terms of from $20,000,000 to $25,000,000 a year, whereas in 1952 the Foundation gave away $38,000,000, in 1953 $59,000,000, and in 1954 $68,000,000. The only way it has been able to continue operating without greatly expanding its payroll has been to dispose of from half to three-quarters of its income each year in huge chunks to its various Funds, in massive grants like last year's $2,000,000 to the Harvard Business School, and in projects on the scale of its current attempt to raise college teachers' salaries. "The first thing you have to do every year is get rid of most of your income in a few very big operations," says one of the Ford Foundation's vice-presidents. "Then you're down to Rockefeller size—around twenty million a year—

and you can begin to act like a foundation instead of like the United States Treasury. This teacher's-salary program looks very promising, very promising."

Some philanthropoids in other foundations, while acknowledging the Ford Foundation's problem, feel that it could have been solved better. They think that, especially in the Hoffman-Hutchins period, the Foundation gave too much and too soon. "It's hard to give away a lot of money without doing harm," one of them observed not long ago. "You might increase growth too suddenly, causing the grantee to enlarge his staff, set up branch offices, et cetera, out of all proportion to his normal rate of development, and first thing you know you have organizational cancer." He felt that the Foundation had been too eager to make a big splash right away, and he was unimpressed by the excuse often given for some of the boners of the Hoffman regime—that it had to get rid of a lot of money fast. "They could have picked a half-dozen small, first-rate colleges and divided up two-thirds of their annual budget among them for a couple of years," he added. "This would have meant a lot to each college. The other third could have gone into their own ideas, beginning small, building up a staff—that takes time—and constantly revising until they got something that really worked. If they made mistakes, at least they would have been small ones." In the same vein, another non-Ford philanthropoid pointed out not long ago that the Fund for the Advancement of Education could have introduced its Arkansas Plan, for educating teachers, on a small, experimental scale and then gradually got it accepted. "Instead, they began it dramatically, on a statewide basis, and aroused the maximum opposition. Even under Gaither, the temptation to make a splash isn't always resisted. They announced the first fifty million dollars of that program for raising professors' salaries before they had even written the colleges about it. Academic people first learned about it from the front pages of their newspapers. I got five or six calls myself the next day from deans and presidents, asking what I knew and how they could get their teachers in on the program. There was a lot of confusion and even some bad feeling. I understand that the trustees insisted on announcing it, over the staff's objections. Trustees always want to grab headlines. But the staff should have been able to control their trustees better."

All this is merely the practical side of the problem, however. There is another aspect, more subtle and probably insoluble. When philanthropy goes into mass production, it tends to become routine. Feeling, imagination, and even reality begin to leak away. Personally, the philanthropoids at Ford are decent enough fellows of reasonably high intelligence, but they are caught in the gears of a $2,500,000,000 mechanism. The most frequent complaint of those who have tried to interest the Foundation in a project—and it is one that has been made even by successful applicants—is remarkably similar to what one hears about Hollywood, another organism that is muscle-bound with money: They had the feeling that they were not dealing with people but were up against an intricate slot machine that might pay off or might not, according to its own arcane mechanical logic. The conscientious philanthropoid at 477 Madison must also feel this kind of frustration at times. The Foundation's money often, perhaps usually, does good to actual flesh-and-blood people after it has at last filtered down to them through the proper channels, but from the top of the great machine, which is where the philanthropoid is perched, this is not so evident. He is likely to be as surprised as he is pleased when, during a trip into "the field," he sees the human good done by the millions he has been disbursing. But when the philanthropoid climbs back up into his seat of power, his desk chair, he becomes a victim of the scale on which he must operate, and his life is once more a matter of processing grants, allocating subsidies, and committing funds to implement well-rounded programs. Then he reverts to foundationese, a language that abstracts from reality enough of its life, variety, and general sloppiness to allow it to be embalmed in a staff memorandum. "Foundations are like sacrifices without salt," wrote Francis Bacon, "merely the painted sepulchres of alms, which soon will putrefy and corrupt inwardly."

Then there is the problem, connected with bigness, of what is euphemistically called collective scholarship. Nothing is more often criticized about Ford and the other large foundations than their tendency to favor research teams over individual inquiry. Abraham Flexner quotes Einstein approvingly: "I am a horse for single harness, not cut out for tandem or teamwork; for well I know that in order to attain any definite goal, it is imperative that *one* person should do the thinking and commanding." (Flexner might also have cited his own classic 1910 survey of North American medical schools.) "The great inventive minds [in the social sciences]—Plato, Hobbes, Rousseau, Hegel, Bentham —do not seem to have been natural members of committees," Harold Laski, who could hardly have been accused of an unsympathetic attitude toward Progress, once wrote. "Coöperative research . . . seems to me to raise hopes unlikely of fulfillment. It is an immense superstructure without due bedrock in the facts of intellectual creativeness."

There is, in short, a widespread suspicion that constructive thinking can take place only inside one skull at a time, and that the enforced collectivization of thought, far from producing more or better ideas, merely brings everything down to the safely mediocre. "No effective substitute has been or is likely to be found for the individual human mind as an instrument for making fundamentally new discoveries." So runs the first sentence of Elbridge Sibley's *Support for Independent Scholarship and Research* (Social Science Research Council, 1951), an acute—and saddening —study of the plight of the "lone-wolf" scholar. Nevertheless, team thinking has become the dominant academic pattern. "Quantitative research in all fields today is conducted by groups of workers," a prominent economic theorist recently wrote, apropos of a project the Foundation had asked his opinion on. "The process by which a group of scientific men evolve a joint integrated problem of research is impeded by the presence of the obdurate lone worker. It seems to me that learning to work in teams is one important function of this project because students trained in empirical work will ordinarily find employment only in group situations."

President Gaither, who is defensive about the question, as are most philanthropoids, says the foundations are simply following the lead of the universities, and adds that the government gave a great impetus to the trend during the war by spreading enormous research contracts throughout the academic world. (Some universities now take in more from contract research than in tuition fees.) "We do try to take care of the individual," Gaither insists, "but it's hard in a foundation of this size." A big foundation, for technical reasons, must spend the bulk of its money on big projects, which, in the academic world, mean team projects. Several years ago, while he was president of the Carnegie Corporation, Charles Dollard explained to a Congressional committee why this is so:

My first job in the Corporation was to handle a program of grants to individuals, which I did from 1938 to 1942. It was not, as far as we were concerned, a successful program. . . . It takes more careful study, more careful investigation to make a grant of $5,000 to one individual than it does to give a grant of a half million to a well-established university, because in one case you have to get all of your facts yourself, in the other case the facts are very readily available, and, indeed, you will start with a good deal of knowledge about the institution.

It can take as much staff work to give a $3,500 Guggenheim Fellowship as to give $3,500,000 to a well-known institution. More staff work demands a larger staff, which would mean that if Ford tried to give away most of its $60,000,000 a year to individuals, it would have to expand its staff greatly, with all the dangers of bureaucratism that this implies. (Guggenheim, which alone among the large foundations gives grants only to individuals, spends a mere $1,000,000 a year.) It would also mean that the influence of the Ford Foundation on our culture would be enormously increased, since it would have to decide in detail just which individual projects should be encouraged and which not, instead of giving large sums to other institutions and letting *them* decide how to spend the money, as it does now. Those who advocate more spending on individuals, however, see no harm in foundations' exerting more influence if it is a healthy one. They also feel that if the big foundations were more *au courant* with current intellectual developments than they seem to be, they could pick out the talented individuals without a great deal of red tape and investigation. It takes a mind to spot a mind, and the modern philanthropoid is an executive or a diplomat or a front man but rarely an intellectual. Ezra Pound, the very model of a modern intellectual, wrote to Simon Guggenheim in 1925: "Dear Sir: Permit me to congratulate you on the terms in which your Memorial Foundation is announced. For the first time I see an endowment that seems to have a chance of being effective. That is to say, the terms of the announcement do not of necessity imply defeat of the announced object. . . . The only way to make a civilization is to exploit to the full those individuals who happen to be given by nature the aptitudes, exceptional aptitudes, for particular jobs. By exploit I mean that they must be allowed to do the few things which they and no one else can." But it is hard to imagine Mr. Pound in a foundation.

In his thoughtful *Fortune* article "Where the Foundations Fall Down," William H. Whyte, Jr., after describing the "bureaucratization" of the social sciences by the increasing pressure for group projects, continues, "And how have the foundations responded? They are not countering the bureaucratization of research; they are intensifying it. In making grants, they channel the bulk of their money to large-scale team projects and programs. . . . Academics joke privately (and bitterly) that it's easier to get $500,000 from a foundation than $5,000; understandably, many react by inflating their projects, and the more they do so, the more satisfied the foundations are that their way of giving is the proper way." The result is that it is steadily becoming harder for an American professor to be a scholar—as against, if he is eminent, a project administrator or, if he is young and unknown, a research assistant—because the essential equipment for scholarship is too cheap to be interesting to foundations, being no more than one man's living expenses, plus paper, pencils, and access to a library. "Right now I have an idea that's worth a middling-sized project, but I'm not going to apply," Whyte quotes one social scientist as saying. "What I would enjoy would be the broad exploratory part, but if I worked up the project, I'd get involved in administration. I would have to spend a year organizing a research design that would please the foundation people."

Paul Weiss, Professor of Philosophy at Yale and author of *Nature and Man* and other books, recently wrote a friend:

> In the realm of money as well as in the realm of ideas, the individual stands somewhat opposed to the institution. They have different values, rhythms, stresses. In the end, the individual must defy the very organizations that are presumably designed to help him.
>
> I was once asked by a foundation head for suggestions. He took out his pen. I said, "Help struggling young men." He said, "Who?" I gave him the names of several young, unknown men who needed a few hundred dollars to complete a book, hire a typist, etc. He put his pen back in his pocket, got up, and that was the end of that.

In short, there seems to be a mutual repulsion between the creative individual and large sums of money, and since culture is produced by individuals and not by committees or teams or boards or bureaus, this means that the large foundations are in the absurd position of having too much money to be able to promote cultural growth and experiment. It is like trying to pick up a pin while wearing boxing gloves.

There is something boring, unsatisfying, even irritating about the work of a great modern foundation like Ford. It is hard to see at first glance why this should be so. Only a misanthrope of heroic proportions could object to the giving away of money to help needy students through college or to explore some aspect of human behavior or to raise the living standard of Indian peasants. Yet the feeling persists, even among the philanthropoids themselves. They complain mostly of a curious sense of unreality. "It was a great satisfaction to get back to a profit-and-loss statement," Hoffman remarked after he had returned to Studebaker. "Now I know just where I am every month. Never did at the Foundation." A former Hoffman associate at Ford, who is now a professor, recalls that while he was with the Foundation he felt he was in a never-never land. "There weren't any of the ordinary bench marks that people can use in real life to see how they're doing," he says. "You work up in the stratosphere with money that isn't yours—that isn't anybody's, really— and there's no way of telling whether you're using it wisely or not, because there's no competition, no criticism. You won't get fired if you fail—and anyway nobody could be sure that you *were* failing. No one ever got fired from a foundation for doing a bad job—only for sticking to a principle." Beardsley Ruml, as, successively, executive head of the Laura Spelman Rockefeller Memorial, dean of the social sciences at the University of Chicago, and chairman of R. H. Macy & Co., has had experience in the foundation, the academic, and the business worlds. ("He's giving up ideas for notions," Hutchins observed apropos Ruml's migration to Macy's.) As far as he is concerned, the foundation world was by all odds the most frustrating. "You're operating in a vacuum," he says. "You never know what people think of your work, because no one will tell you with any frankness. Even the people you turn down won't criticize you to your face if they have any hope of getting a grant later—and most of them do—though of course there's plenty of private backbiting and grumbling. It's all very corrupting and gives you a feeling of complete insecurity."

Even the most iconoclastic young scholar hesitates to say anything unfavorable about a large foundation; he is either grateful for past favors or hopeful of future ones. It seems to be as hard for a foundation to get anyone to criticize it seriously as it is easy for it to stimulate attacks from people with large political axes to grind. Indeed, almost the only way a foundation can subject itself to valid criticism is to pay for it; Ford often hires consulting experts to appraise its projects. Writing of the foundation executive, Harold Laski observed, "He travels luxuriously, is amply entertained wherever he goes (he has so much to give), and he speaks always to hearers keenly alert to sense the direction of his own interests in order that they may explain that this is the one thing they are anxious to develop in their own university. When you see him at a college, it is like nothing so much as the vision of an important customer in a department store. Deferential salesmen surround him on every hand, anticipating his every wish, alive to the importance of his good opinion, fearful lest he be dissatisfied and go to their rival across the way. . . . The foundations do not control, simply because, in the direct and simple sense of the word, there is no need for them to do so. They have only to indicate the immediate direction of their minds for the whole university to discover that it always meant to gravitate swifty to that angle of the intellectual compass." The dilemma confronting the philanthropoid is that of King Midas—his golden touch robs everything of its natural qualities.

Another boring thing about a big foundation is the money, which is, so to speak, sterilized. Reformers used to denounce Rockefeller's "tainted money"—the phrase now has an old-fashioned creak—but foundation money today would be more interesting if it weren't so pure. It was a human action, and therefore one capable of arousing admiration, disgust, aversion, sympathy, or some other emotion, for the Medicis to spend their gold, soiled with blood and sharp practice, on artists whose work they themselves enjoyed, or for Carnegie, disposing of the millions he had made by less violent but equally dubious methods, to announce that he felt like giving away libraries, or, later, to run his Carnegie Corporation himself. (Its executive committee during his lifetime consisted of himself and his two personal secretaries.) But when Henry and Edsel Ford died and left ninety per cent of their Ford stock to their Foundation, the money was, in effect, socialized; that is, purged of all personal interest and converted into a fund "for the public welfare," to be administered by bureaucrats who are supposed not to have any whims or enthusiasms of their own but simply to weigh everything dispassionately on the scales of "the general welfare." This is doubtless an advance in social justice, but it doesn't make for interest. Nor is it even certain that it makes for efficiency. An individual who has a passion, an interest, a hobby, or perhaps only a whim, and who is able to indulge it freely just as he likes, can often pick out the thinker or the artist most likely to gratify his taste, while a committee, deprived by definition of his singleness of purpose and vision, flounders around in the dark night of collective evaluation and finally comes out with a compromise on either one big, and hence safe, name, or a dozen little names, of which, it is hoped, two or three will pan out. The amateur—the very word is now a sneer, since it means someone who cares for painting or chemistry or whatnot, and these days personal feeling takes a back seat to objective knowledge— from Maecenas, the patron and friend of Vergil and Horace, to the rich American lady who helped support Joyce while he was writing *Ulysses*, has a record of success at least as impressive as that of the university and foundation committees of our day, including the one that gives out Guggenheim Fellowships. "They are only workers in the vineyard," says Ruml of the philanthropoids. "They didn't plant the vines and they won't drink the wine."

Two centuries ago, Turgot complained of the inability of the original donor to "communicate his own zeal from age to age," while Adam Smith wrote, "The effect of endowment on those entrusted with any cause is necessarily soporific." The modern philanthropoid is zealous, or at least wideawake, for, after all, his job has become a profession instead of a drowsy sinecure, as it was in the eighteenth century, but he does feel something impersonal, and therefore unreal, about his work. This impersonality has several unexpected results. One is a curious resentment it seems to create in people against an institution that operates entirely for their own good—a sentiment like that of the Athenian who voted to ostracize Aristides because he was tired of hearing him called "The Just." An eccentric who gives away money to gratify a whim, or even a base man who gives it away out of vanity or even less admirable motives, is not as irritating as a perfectly just man who gives on the basis of knowing what will be best for other people. "We don't want to play God," an earnest Ford philanthropoid explained at a party. "We only want to diffuse creativity and thought." A second result is that since no one individual's taste or intelligence can be dominant in a large foundation (a notable exception to this as to most other generalizations about the modern foundation was the Hoffman-Hutchins regime at Ford), there is a tendency toward the mediocre, the mean level of the board or committee that is making the decision. "New proposals are passed around among a large staff," observed the late Edwin R. Embree, who was president of the Julius Rosenwald Fund for twenty years. "To get by the doubts of half a dozen distinguished and self-important critics, a proposal has to be so 'sound' as to be almost innocuous."

In another letter—to Harriet Monroe, in 1927—Ezra Pound, a master of counter-foundationese, gets to the point:

I have never contended that the American millionaire or "ploot" was an idiot. I have said and still maintain that he is an uncivilized barbarian usually unpleasant and never interested in the arts. He will endow any number of "institutions" employing any number of boneheaded dullards with "degrees," in order that they may still further befuddle the young. He will, in rarer cases, express his dislike of the arts by committees. . . .

And in proof of bluff we have but to observe the "hardheaded" American business man when really interested in something and wishing to improve the quality of creation. Thus *Time* for Aug. 8 re Col. E. H. R. Green (son of Hetty) who is interested in aviation. Sic loquitur Green: "I want young fellows with good ideas and no money . . . to feel that there is a place where they can come. I will grub-stake them when their ideas appear sound and let them perfect and experiment. If they develop anything marketable, they can take it out and it is theirs."

That is to say he knows what he wants, he expects to be interested in seeing it happen *now* and not in A.D. 2547 under the auspices of a committee appointed by the trustees. He is not making a collection of the extant fragments of the war-machinery found in Byzantium or of models of Leonardo's project for a monoplane. Neither does he expect to have apoplectic stroke when some fellow invents something he hadn't thought of. Q.E.D. (*The Letters of Ezra Pound, 1907–1941*, edited by D. D. Paige, Harcourt, Brace, 1950, p. 212.)

Finally, the fact that the modern foundation is the impersonal trustee of money that nobody really "owns" means that it must be able to account for its grants, to defend them, in a way that an individual donor would not have to. If Henry Ford had given $100,000,000 one year to Harvard—to use an obviously fictitious example—the general reaction, even among those who didn't like Harvard, would have been: It's his money, and he can spend it any way he wants to. But if the Foundation he somewhat unwittingly founded were to do this, there would be protests everywhere—Why so much to Harvard? Are there not other equally deserving universities? What right has a foundation to change the educational pattern? And at once a covey of senators from the Middle and Far West would demand an investigation.

This, among other things, explains the timidity of the great foundations in the face of criticism from the public, the press, and Congress—they are almost as public-relations conscious as the great corporations—and also their reluctance to go very far in encouraging the new and untried. "It's hard to be daring in a big foundation," Ford trustee McCloy has remarked. "You're constantly being forced into conventional grooves by criticism or the fear of it. But some of the things Paul Hoffman did rang round the world." And it does seem to be a fact that during its two years under Hoffman, a wide-ranging crusader who surrounded himself with some very unphilanthropoidal types, the Foundation managed to express to some extent the enthusiasms—and the illusions—of him and his colleagues, and therefore was in that brief period more daring and interesting than a self-respecting foundation has any right to be. It was also, on occasion, more foolish. But all that is being taken care of now, for better and for worse, by President Gaither and his conscientious philanthropoids.

CHAPTER 6

ANCIENT HISTORY

THE FORD FOUNDATION began life in a small way
in Detroit in 1936. Its original endowment was a $25,000
check from Edsel Ford and its articles of incorporation
ran to just three typed pages. Both its cash and its verbosity
have increased considerably since then. Its history divides
naturally into two parts—a provincial period, which lasted
up to 1950, and its present modern, or global, era. In the
fourteen years of its provincial phase, the Foundation gave
away a total of $19,000,000, or less than a third of what it
spent in 1954 and less than a thirtieth of the $600,000,000
plus that, in 1955, it committed itself to giving away in
the near future. The $19,000,000 was doled out, at the rate
of a mere $1,000,000 or so a year, to a number of local
worthy causes, such as the Detroit Symphony, in which
the Edsel Fords were interested; the Henry Ford Hospital;
and two remarkable monuments to that antiquarian passion
that so oddly complemented industrial genius in the first
Ford's personality—almost as though he were unconsciously
trying to preserve with one hand what he had destroyed
with the other. One of these is the fascinating Henry Ford
Museum, in Dearborn, where fourteen acres of old loco-
motives. trolley cars, churns, buggies, dresses, lamps, air-

planes, automobiles, sleighs, plows, steam engines, printing presses, lathes, toys, harnesses, pressed glass, Colonial furniture, and other American artifacts are housed behind a front made up of replicas of the façades of three famous Philadelphia buildings (Congress Hall, the Old City Hall, and Independence Hall). The other monument is the adjacent Greenfield Village, among whose hundred or so historic, or at least venerable, structures are Edison's laboratory from Menlo Park, New Jersey, the shed in which the first Ford was built, and the birthplaces of Noah Webster, Luther Burbank, the Wright Brothers, and William H. McGuffey, the author of *McGuffey's Readers.*

In its provincial period, the Foundation was of minor concern even to the Ford family. Unlike Carnegie and Rockefeller, Henry Ford never showed much interest in philanthropy. "Give the average man something and you make an enemy of him," he once remarked. Although in 1930 he told a reporter that he "wanted to do everything he could to help young men fit themselves for the world," adding that he planned to devote the rest of his life to education and might spend "perhaps $100,000,000" in "developing his ideas," this seems to have been one of those impulsive off-the-cuff pronunciamentos with which he liked to flutter the press from time to time. There is some doubt, also, as to how far his ideas would have proved capable of development; "Mr. Ford," concluded the report, "said he believed every youth should learn a trade, to keep him active and out of trouble." In any case, except for a few highly idiosyncratic ventures like the Ford Museum, Greenfield Village, the Peace Ship, and the restoration of Longfellow's Wayside Inn, the elder Ford's concept of philanthropy was pretty much limited to giving away Ford cars in somewhat the same casual way that the elder Rockefeller used to hand out dimes. "I don't recall the Foundation ever being discussed at home," says Henry Ford II.

The family attitude began to change, however, with the death of Edsel Ford, in 1943, and it changed even more with the death of Henry himself, in 1947. It then became evident that the family lawyers who had drawn up the articles of incorporation in 1936 had had something more in mind than the accumulation of old churns and trolley cars. Between them, the father and the son had owned practically all the stock of the Ford Motor Company, which was by far the largest privately owned corporation in the country. So private was the Ford Motor Company that up to the end of 1955 it had never made public a balance sheet or an earnings statement. The Ford Foundation, from the point of view of the family and its lawyers, was a device, as simple and efficient as the Model T, for perpetuating this privacy in the face of death and taxes. Henry and Edsel left ten per cent of their Ford stock to their heirs: Mrs. Henry Ford, Mrs. Edsel Ford, and the Edsel Fords' four children—a daughter, who is married to an unrelated Ford, and three sons, Henry II, Benson, and William Clay. All the remaining ninety per cent of the stock went to the Foundation. Had it gone to the heirs, they would have had to pay inheritance taxes of about seventy-seven per cent, or some $321,000,000 (figuring the stock at $135 a share, the extremely moderate valuation accepted by the government in settling the estate). To realize such a sum, the heirs would have had to sell all or most of the stock—a move that at best would have meant admitting outsiders into the company and at worst actually losing control. The lawyers forestalled another threat to privacy by including all the voting stock in the heirs' ten per cent. Thus the Foundation, in spite of holding ninety per cent of the stock, had no voice in the management; it was a pensioner, not a partner. Whether coincidentally or not, Ford Motors since 1950 has paid out in dividends only about half as much of its profits as General Motors and Chrysler, which are controlled by far-flung thousands of stockholders with full voting powers and a consequent ability to insist on a more generous dividend policy. This has enabled Ford to put a greater proportion of its profits into plant and equipment, a competitive advantage that is viewed with a fishy eye by other automobile manufacturers. The Ford family's lawyers, finally, saw to it that their clients did not have to pay the inheritance tax on the shares they *did* inherit. Henry's and Edsel's wills provided that the bequests to the members of the family be tax-free, thereby, in effect, imposing the entire tax burden on what was left to the Ford Foundation. The tax bill came to $42,063,725, which was about equal to the total spent by the Foundation on all its benevolences through 1950. Sweet are the uses of philanthropy.

Such a convenient solution of the Ford family's business problems could hardly be expected to endure forever, for various reasons. One is that it is obviously not wise for the Foundation to keep all its investment eggs in one basket; the much smaller resources of the Carnegie and Rockefeller foundations are spread among dozens of corporations. Another is that Washington doesn't approve of the use of a foundation to retain control of a business; the House Ways and Means Committee in 1950 suggested that foundations whose endowments consist largely of the stock of one closely held company should lose their tax exemption, and although Congress did not act on the suggestion then, there is no certainty that it won't in the future. "Last year, during the futile search of Representative B. Carroll Reece, the Tennessee Republican, for evidence of subversive tendencies in the Ford Foundation and other tax-free philanthropic institutions, many Wall Street observers said there was a more valid criticism of the Foundation," the *Times* financial page noted not long ago. "This was that its assets . . . invested in Ford stock perpetuated a privileged fiscal position not subject to public scrutiny." A third reason is the one already mentioned—the resentment of competitors at the freedom Ford Motors enjoys from pressure for bigger dividends. "No other automobile manufacturer is in a position to ignore stability of earnings or continuity of dividend payments," the *Corporate Director*, a business monthly, stated in its issue of April, 1954, in the course of a rather acidulous review of Ford's comfortable competitive position. "If General Motors or Chrysler earned no money and paid no dividends this year, management heads would roll and equity credit would be seriously impaired. . . . It is our belief that in this case and in many others Federal legislation is needed that will prohibit any charitable foundation . . . from owning more than ten per cent of any business enterprise. . . . Otherwise, the public has no voice in the company, and the profit motive cannot survive due to the great advantage enjoyed by companies that can offer unfair competition." Still another reason was recently suggested by Raymond Moley in *Newsweek* —that the more of its Ford stock the Foundation sells off, the less will Ford Motors be "involved in the controversies in which the Foundation has been involved from its beginning." Since these controversies—or, more accurately, attacks—are as virulent and widespread now as ever and show no sign of abating, the brothers Ford may be presumed to be not averse to a greater separation of their business life from their philanthropic life.

For a long time, therefore, the problem of selling some of the Foundation's Ford stock was in the hands of a committee of trustees composed of President Gaither and Messrs. Brownlee, McCloy, and Wilson. Finally, in November of 1955, the Foundation announced that it was going to sell fifteen per cent of its holdings in Ford. The trustees' committee had not had to spend much time worrying about how to create a market for the stock. Chairman Breech of Ford Motors had reported that the company had made more money in the first three quarters of 1955 than in any previous full year, and competition among brokers for a chance to handle some of the issue—722 were included in the syndicate, one of the many quantitative records set by the whole transaction—and among investors for a chance to buy a few shares at the initial offering price, reached bargain-counter intensity. So intense, indeed, that the Foundation the next month increased the percentage of its Ford shares it was putting on the market from fifteen to twenty-two, partly because it seemed a pity not to cash in as much as possible on the current passion to own Ford stock, partly as a matter of public relations, to avoid disappointing people and to spread the ownership of Ford Motors as democratically far and wide as possible. (Those who are in control of a company are always in favor of the most democratic levelling-down process in the composition of the other stockholdings.) In December, 1955, Ford Motors made public for the first time its earnings and profits, as required by the regulations of the Securities and Exchange Commission. The figures were even larger than had been anticipated—net earnings for the first nine months of 1955, for instance, were $312,200,000 and sales were over $4 billion—and when, the following month, the Foundation's stock went on sale, it brought in some $643,000,000.

What bothered the trustees' committee, and demanded a good deal of both its time and its ingenuity, was nothing so crude as how to sell the stock. It was, rather, the delicate matter of voting rights. The difficulty was that if the stock was to have a wide market—desirable, since the Foundation plans to sell off a lot more of its Ford shares later—it would have to be listed on the New York Stock Exchange; this meant that the Ford family would have to give the public not only a voice in management but a majority voice, because the Exchange requires that for such an issue to be listed, the shares available on the market must add up to a majority of the voting stock. This was worked out by a complicated revision of the company's capital structure which gave the twenty-two per cent of its stock that the

Foundation sold sixty per cent of the total voting power, the remaining forty per cent being retained by the Ford family's holdings. An ambitious investor, or group of investors, with $650,000,000 or so lying around could therefore, when the stock went on sale, have seized majority control of Ford by buying only about twenty per cent of the company's stock.

Nothing of the sort happened, of course—and even had such an industrial imperialist been around, his style would have been fatally cramped by the Foundation's super-democratic requirement that all orders for 100 or less shares had to be filled before any larger ones were. So the Ford family's forty per cent of the voting power still comfortably dominates the board of directors—in a large corporation ten per cent usually gives working control. The stock the Foundation is keeping will still be without voting rights, but when, or if, more of it is sold, the shares already on the market will have their voting power reduced enough to give the new shares a pro-rata part of the sixty per cent of the voting power that is to be, so to speak, reserved for the public.

The Messrs. Gaither, Brownlee, McCloy, and Wilson also worried a good deal about what to do with the proceeds of the sale. This problem threatened to be even more complex than the first question was. Under the headline "FORD FUND FACES CASH INDIGESTION," Robert E. Bedingfield wrote in the *Times* (before the stock had been sold):

Wall Streeters are fully agreed that [reinvesting the money] is likely to prove as difficult as selling Ford stock is going to be easy. Four to five hundred million is almost an unbelievable amount of new money to be invested in corporate securities by one institution. It is five times as much as the Carnegie Corporation . . . had invested in 102 common stocks at the end of 1954. It is . . . more than half as much as the total assets of the Massachusetts Investors Trust at the end of last year.

The latter, the nation's biggest investment company, has been more than three decades developing its huge portfolio.

If the trustees of the Ford Foundation, in their search for diversification, were even to limit their selections to "The Favorite Fifty"—the fifty stocks most favored by more than 175 investment companies—they would create an abnormal demand and push prices to completely unrealistic levels.

Thus, the Foundation's money promised to be as hard to invest as it had been to give away. The trustees' decision, in December, 1955, to give away $500,000,000 by the middle of 1957 to an unselect list of private hospitals, medical schools, and liberal-arts colleges (all there were, to be exact) eased their subcommittee's problem, but there still remains the $150,000,000 or so surplus from the first stock sale plus proceeds of later sales, so that Mr. Bedingfield's forebodings may yet be realized. There's just too much of the stuff around the place.

In 1948, as Henry Ford's estate neared settlement, the trustees of the Foundation began to worry about how they would spend All That Money—even the most pessimistic hardly anticipated the immensity of the flood bearing down on them—in such a way as to command the respect of the public and the tolerance of the tax authorities. The trustees at that time were Henry Ford II, who, as Edsel's eldest son and the head of Ford Motors, was more or less ex-officio chairman of the Foundation; Benson Ford; several family friends; and two outsiders—the late Karl Compton, of M.I.T., and Donald K. David, of the Harvard Business School, who has long been Henry II's most trusted counsellor in philanthropic matters. They came to the not startling conclusion that the first step should be to have a committee make a study. To direct this, the outsiders proposed Gaither, who at the time was a youngish San Francisco lawyer; Ford, who had already met Gaither and had been impressed by him, offered him the job. As Gaither later told a Congressional committee, "He wanted to know what the people of the United States thought this Foundation should use its resources for in the interests of the public welfare, and he knew of no better way than to go out and find out what people thought." This was perhaps naïve—Gaither and his Study Committee talked not to "the people of the United States," of course, but to experts who knew, or thought they knew, what "the people" wanted, or ought to want—but it was sincere. Henry II and his trustees had decided to remodel their Foundation on Carnegie and Rockefeller lines, instead of merely expanding their local spending; that is, they were thinking in national and, indeed, international terms, rather than of using their prospective millions to buttress the interests of Detroit and Ford Motors in the way the Duke Endowment uses its millions for the greater glory of the Carolinas and Duke Power. Since this was the kind of foundation that appealed to Gaither, too, he accepted the job, after making sure that the Fords and their friends would cease to dominate the Foundation. Gaither estimated that the proposed study would require about a year, and when Henry II seemed taken aback, he explained to the neophyte philanthropist, "This is a very big thing and there is no point skimping, to get it right." It was a sound, if elementary, lesson: In philanthropy, velocity is inversely proportionate to mass.

Gaither and his collaborators travelled 250,000 miles, talked with over 1,000 experts, and produced an enormous quantity of mimeographed reports. (Those on education alone came to 3,400 pages.) The final result was an expensively printed, 139-page quarto entitled *Report of the Study for the Ford Foundation on Policy and Program*, which is a sacred text around the Foundation's offices and is "believed [by the trustees] to represent the best thinking in the United States today." It is a work of awesome earnestness, composed in the most stately foundationese, where meaning, such as it is, decently drapes itself in Latin-root polysyllables to produce expressions like "organizational prerogatives," "intercultural understanding," "evaluation," "clarification," "constructive recommendations," and "the dissemination of democratic ideals." Along with most other users of this contemporary dead language, the authors of the Study Report show little aversion to the obvious. "In the Committee's opinion," they conclude after their 250,000 miles and 1,000 experts, "the evidence points to the fact that today's most critical problems are those which are social rather than physical in character—those which arise in man's relation to man rather than in his relation to nature." As to the remedy, they venture to speculate: "The problems of mankind must be solved, if they are to be solved at all, by a combined use of all those types of knowledge by which human affairs may be influenced." This seems likely. Their recommendations are set forth in the form of five Program Areas, which are formulated with that "positive" accent that is a specialty of the American public-relations expert: "I. The Establishment of Peace" (international programs; "peace" means trying to make other nations more friendly to us and less to the Communists); "II. The Strengthening of Democracy" (civil liberties, politics); "III. The Strengthening of the Economy" (economics); "IV. Education in a Democratic Society" (the "democratic society" is apparently ours); "V. Individual Behavior and Human Relations" (the "behavioral," or social, sciences, an Area for which a more accurate heading would have been "Mass Behavior and Social Relations"). The scope of the Study Report is even vaster than these Areas suggest. Subhead F, Area III, for example, is nothing less than "the improvement of the standard of living and the economic status of peoples throughout the world," while Subhead A, Area IV, is, quite simply, "the discovery, support, and use of talent and leadership in all fields and at all ages." Analytical precision was not the forte of the authors of the Study Report; Subhead F above could plainly go just as well under Area I, while Subhead A might go under any or all of the five Areas. As one applicant for a grant remarked after struggling through the mazes of the Foundation's Areas, "Trying to decide whether a project fits into this or that Area is like wondering whether to go abroad next winter or by plane."

This heady prospectus, comparable in aspiration, if not intellectual content, to the visions of eighteenth-century Encyclopedists and nineteenth-century Utopians, was submitted to the trustees in the fall of 1949 as the program of the new and greater Ford Foundation. Getting the right man to carry it out was an intricate and lengthy essay in public relations. He had to be a Name who was *persona grata* both to the business community and to the Truman administrtaion, someone who was reasonably liberal and conservatively reasonable and also, if possible, experienced in spending large sums for social purposes. This unlikely creature was found in the person of Paul Hoffman, a former president of the Studebaker Corporation, who had been the main force behind the Committee for Economic Development, a group of liberalistic business leaders, and who was then spending several billions of the taxpayers' money as administrator of the Marshall Plan. After prolonged negotiations—"I kept trying because I knew he was the man for the job," Henry Ford II said when they were over—Hoffman agreed to head the Foundation, but for various reasons, official and personal, including an act of God in the form of a gall-bladder operation, he was unable to take office until January, 1951. This was more than two years after the Study Report had been begun.

The delay was unnerving to the trustees, and still more so to their lawyers, for Ford Motors, rejuvenated by the new management Henry II had installed, was now producing profits at an alarming rate. In 1948 and 1949, the Foundation had received in dividends the appalling sum of

$50,000,000, of which the trustees, used to the small-time tempo of $1,000,000 or so a year, were able to spend only a tenth. The Internal Revenue Bureau was becoming restive. Also, in 1948 the late Senator Charles W. Tobey, of New Hampshire, whose talent for public indignation was soon to have a wider field in the Kefauver Crime Committee, investigated foundations as tax-avoiding mechanisms. Although the Senator occupied himself mostly with Royal Little and the New England textile empire he had whipped up by using foundations as reservoirs of tax-free capital, no one knew when the Senator's crusading eye might focus on the Ford Foundation. And in 1950 the House Ways and Means Committee held hearings on various proposals, including some by Senator Tobey, to tighten up on tax exemption for foundations. Out of these hearings came a section of the 1950 Revenue Act forbidding "unreasonable" accumulation of income by foundations. The Act failed to define "unreasonable," but the general feeling among lawyers was that the courts would look askance at any foundation that failed to spend at least seventy per cent of its income each year. By this standard, the Ford Foundation was not doing brilliantly. In 1950, the uncontrollably profitable Ford Motor Company embarrassed the Foundation with $87,000,000 more in dividends. Even by such heroic, and slightly desperate, efforts as giving $14,000,000 to the Ford Hospital and $6,000,000 to the Edison Institute, the trustees were unable to spend as much as a third of their 1950 income, let alone make a dent in the $45,000,000 surplus that had piled up in the preceding two years. The Foundation's 1950 Report, while admitting that recent dividends had been "relatively large," hopefully predicted, "In 1951 and the foreseeable future, a reduction in such income is anticipated because of the national emergency, with reduced volume of automobile production." Although income in the next two years did fall off to a mere $32,000,000 a year, as a consequence of the Korean war, it rose to $48,000,000 in 1953 and has continued to rise ever since. On top of all the other problems a foundation is heir to, the Ford trustees and staff have been chronically beset by the brute necessity of keeping abreast of an income that has been piling up higher and faster than anything known up to now in the history of foundations.

When Hoffman took over at the beginning of 1951 and moved the Foundation's headquarters from Detroit to Pasadena, California, it was in an atmosphere reminiscent of Franklin Roosevelt's "hundred days" in 1933—one of crisis and opportunity, doom and enthusiasm. Both the international situation and the Foundation's own tax problem called for large spending quickly. No one knew when, or if, the Korean war would explode into a third world war; reforms had to be swift and extensive if they were to make any difference. "We all felt the world had to be saved by next Tuesday," a Foundation veteran of that expansive era has recalled, adding professionally, "We had a crisis orientation." There was no lack of confidence that the crisis could be dealt with. "We will appoint a group of experts to identify problems for which we will find the answers," Hoffman announced. His own pet project was an investigation into the conditions of peace, which he described in an unpublished interview:

The world can't go on indefinitely this way. You are either going to have a war or peace, and I think we all want peace. What we have to know are the conditions that must be created to make such a peace possible. There are some things Russia must do and some we must do and some the other countries must do, but we don't know what they are. If we could find out what they are, maybe there would be some way of doing them. I asked Jack McCloy [who had just resigned as United States High Commissioner for Germany] to take on the job and he said he didn't want to do it—it was too vague. But I talked him into it, and he has been at it for a while, and just a few days ago he told me he was getting his teeth into it and it wasn't so vague any more. Maybe he will come up with something—I don't know. Or maybe Grenny Clark [Grenville Clark, an eminent lawyer and elder statesman] has something in his plan for Universal Disarmament. I don't know about that, either, but it's worth supporting. We feel that if you get good men and supply them with funds, you must be doing a good thing.

Nothing much came of McCloy's or Clark's labors (except a 149-page brochure by the latter, proposing a number of revisions in the charter of the United Nations, from which something may or may not come when the U.N. may or may not decide to revise its charter), possibly because the problems involved were a bit outsize even for good men liberally supplied with funds. As the editorial writer of the Council Bluffs, Iowa, *Nonpareil* observed, apropos the Foundation, in the issue of October 7, 1951: "Every year it becomes more apparent that money will not save the world."

The first person Hoffman got in to help him manage the Foundation, as an associate director, was Robert Maynard Hutchins, for whom he had conceived a high regard while serving as a trustee of the University of Chicago when the latter was Chancellor of the institution. There were three other associate directors: Gaither; Chester C. Davis, a St. Louis banker and farm expert who had been the head of the Agricultural Adjustment Administration during the New Deal; and Milton Katz, a Harvard Law School professor who had served as Hoffman's deputy in carrying out the Marshall Plan. But it was Hoffman and Hutchins who ran the main show. Both were men of extremely large ideas and both were accomplished at spending extremely large sums of money. Of the $60,000,000 spent by the Foundation in the two years—1951 and 1952—that Hoffman and Hutchins ran it, $21,000,000 went into an international program that was worked out mainly by

Hoffman, on the basis of his own administrative experience in Europe and of what he had learned in the course of an Asiatic tour during which he conferred with Nehru and other leaders, while $33,000,000 went into the two great Funds that Hutchins persuaded the trustees to establish—the Fund for the Advancement of Education and the Fund for Adult Education. Between them, Hoffman and Hutchins fixed a pattern of spending that only began to change radically last year. But the atmosphere—the mood—has changed a great deal and did so much earlier. It is, for instance, quite impossible to imagine any of the high officers of the Foundation today—or, for that matter, any of the sober professionals who run the other big foundations—dashing off the sort of verses with which the amateurs of the Hoffman-Hutchins era relieved their souls on occasion. Martin Quigley, a high-spirited fellow who was then in charge of the publicity department at Pasadena headquarters, wrote "Philanthropic Stew, a Recipe Derived from an Annual Report of the Ford Foundation, Circa 1952," which runs, in part:

Take a dozen Quakers—be sure they're sweet and pink—
Add one discussion program to make the people think;
Brown a liberal education in television grease
And roll in economics, seasoned well with peace.
Crush a juvenile delinquent (or any wayward kid)
And blend it with the roots of an Asiatic's id.
Dice teachers' education, and in a separate pan
Make a sauce of brown technicians from India-Pakistan
And pour it over seed corn in a pilot demonstration,
One that has been flavored with peel-off implication.
Take a board of good conservatives, the nicest you can buy,
And mix them with the white of a beaten liberal's eye;
Now render the conditions of a peace that's just and free
And mix *them* with insistence on national sovereignty.
Stir everything together, and when the fire's hot,
Pour a little Russian exile into the steaming pot.
Sweeten with publicity all the serving bowls

(By the way, this recipe serves two billion souls),
Garnish with compassion—just a touch will do—
And serve in deep humility your philanthropic stew.

Associate Director Hutchins came up with a special version of "Adeste Fideles":

How firm a Foundation we saints of the Lord
Have built on the faith of our excellent Ford.
We've laundered and lighted the Trustees' report
   And left for California,
   And left for California,
   And left for California,
The place to resort.

How fine a Foundation; we are for peace.
We live peaceful lives, and we hope wars will cease.
We've heard mankind cry, and we've answered the call:
   We're out in Pasadena [*three times*],
Away from it all.

How firm a Foundation; we've three times the dough
And ten times the brains that any other can show.
The hell with Rockefeller and Carnegie, too.
   We've left for California [*three times*],
The hell with you.

The Foundation under Hoffman has been described as a monster with its head in Pasadena, its legs in New York, and its pocketbook in Detroit—a reference to the location in those respective cities of its headquarters, its operating offices, and its treasury. The continental gap between Pasadena and New York contributed to the glorious confusion in which the Foundation often seemed to be operating, but Hoffman had settled in Pasadena, so the Foundation did, too. He and Hutchins may have felt that their new enterprise would be uniquely at home in California, where ideas and oranges both grow big. And, in fact, the state with hot-dog stands modelled on Tintern Abbey was quite at its ease entertaining the Ford Foundation. Samuel Goldwyn visited the luxurious Pasadena estate it had rented for its headquarters, and observed, "If you have to give away money, this is a wonderful place to do it." Applications for grants poured in at such a rate that Hutchins suggested calling the place Itching Palms. The local press frequently celebrated the Foundation with headlines like "FORD FOUNDATION DOLLARS START PEACE FIGHT," "FORD FUND SEEKS DATA ON HUMAN CONDUCT," and "MILLIONS READY TO FURTHER PEACE"—none of which prevented a number of Pasadena housewives from calling up to ask for a fitting. The officers of the Foundation often talked to their fellow-Californians about their hopes and plans, as when Hoffman, Hutchins, and Katz went on a Los Angeles television program on Christmas night in 1951 with a symposium that was described in one of that city's newspapers under the headline "PEACE ON EARTH—IS IT POSSIBLE?" The Ford Foundation, per the Messrs. Hoffman, Hutchins, and Katz, thought it was.

The party ended not with a whimper but a bang, on February 4, 1953, when the trustees fired Hoffman. It was not put exactly that way in the announcement Henry Ford II gave to the press: "Now that the program is well under way, the Trustees—among them Mr. Hoffman—have concluded that administration of the expanding operations of the organization should no longer be divided between New York and Pasadena. . . . The Trustees [have] therefore unanimously agreed to transfer the Pasadena functions to the East. . . . We believe that this move will enable more efficient and economical coördination. . . . While he concurs in this decision, Mr. Hoffman still wishes, for personal reasons, to remain in Pasadena. He has therefore asked to resign as President. . . . This resignation the Trustees have reluctantly accepted." Although it is true that Hoffman was much attached to Pasadena, it is also true that he had been willing to spend a good deal of time abroad while he was running the Marshall Plan and that his present duties as chairman of Studebaker-Packard mean frequent stays in the East. All other things being harmonious, he might have similarly agreed to center his professional life in New York while running the Foundation. All other things were not harmonious, however, although no one around the Foundation cared to disturb the equilibrium of so many millions of dollars consecrated to the welfare of mankind by saying so in public. The press, with more delicacy than enterprise, respected this reticence. Almost the only journalist to suggest that the bag contained a cat was the Hearst society columnist Cholly Knickerbocker, who detected not one but two cats, the first being that Hoffman had resigned because the trustees refused to give Gabriel Pascal $2,000,-000 with which to make a movie about Gandhi, and the second, littered a month later, that "the real story is that Henry Ford II, who at first had great faith in Hoffman, cooled considerably when he realized that Hoffman was working on a scheme that eventually was to put him in control of the entire Ford empire." Athough the bag, in prosaic fact, was innocent of both these particular cats, there were others, their precise size, shape, and color depending on which side is describing them.

Like all defeated factions, from the Gnostic Christians to the Trotskyites, the Hoffmanites are indignant, articulate, and inclined to attribute their downfall to the machinations of overworldly characters. "The Study Report proposed a save-the-world foundation—big men with big ideas," one of them explained not long ago."We gave the trustees what the Report asked for and what they had agreed to, but when they found that big ideas meant criticism, they got scared and wanted to have a safe foundation, like Rockefeller or Carnegie today—one that either makes big grants to respectable, established institutions or a lot of small ones that nobody bothers about. Fred Keppel, of Carnegie, would always give you thirty thousand; it made another line in his annual report and wasn't big enough to upset anyone, or anything. But the Ford Foundation was conceived along more ambitious lines." Although Hoffman himself shows no rancor toward the trustees who fired him—"a very mild incompatibility" is his description of the disagreement—he, also, feels that they were too nervous about criticism. "I told Henry before I took the job that I'm a militant and maybe he didn't really want me," he said recently, and his memory is confirmed by an interview that appeared in 1951 in the *Christian Science Monitor*, in which he said he had told Henry II, "I don't want to be just a banker, watching over a tightly guarded repository from which dollars could be cautiously withdrawn from time to time to meet the needs of well-established and 'safe' charities." Continuing his more recent account of his preëmployment interview with Henry II, Hoffman said, "I told him that I wanted to experiment, to change things, and that change always means trouble. But every time we got a dozen letters objecting to something we'd done—a radio show or an overseas program or whatnot—I'd have to spend hours reassuring the board. I got tired of wasting time that way. I felt I'd done a first-rate job and if, after two years, the trustees didn't agree, I didn't want to have to keep selling them. I'd rather leave."

The trustees are also alleged to have been overconcerned about public relations and correspondingly pained when Hoffman showed no interest in worthy projects that wouldn't have done the Foundation any harm at all. According to the Hoffmanites, Ford Motor Company dealers, of whom there are some 8,200 in the United States, were to blame for much of this kind of pressure; the dealers, they say, couldn't see why a foundation financed by "their" company should spend so much in foreign regions inhabited by few, if any, Ford customers, and kept asking why the Foundation couldn't do good where it would do the most good—to the sale of Ford cars. Those now in control of the Foundation deny that there was such pressure, reporting that when the Ford Motor Company bought and sent a copy of the Foundation's 1953 Report to each Ford dealer, with an invitation to ask questions, the Foundation got just one complaint, from a dealer who objected to grants to Arab nations. There is no doubt, however, that the dealers passed on to Henry II threats to boycott Ford cars made by customers who considered Hoffman and Hutchins wild-eyed One Worlders, if not worse, and who disliked the Foundation's liberalistic flavor. Nothing came of these mutterings, as Ford's record sales in recent years show, but the mere word "boycott" is like a fire bell in the night to any merchandiser. Some of the trustees are also said to have objected to Hoffman's "controversial" personal activities, such as his enthusiasm for the United Nations and UNESCO, his support of ex-Senator Benton when the latter was sued by Senator McCarthy, and his politicking to win the Republican nomination for Eisenhower. "I got the impression intuitively, without anybody's saying so," Hoffman recalls, "that they would feel more comfortable with a good professional administrator who would run the Foundation the way the other big foundations are run and wouldn't get mixed up in extracurricular issues. But my whole idea was to get together men of stature—men of large reputation, who had interests outside the Foundation—and have them operate in a way that was maybe more amateurish than the way the usual anonymous professionals operate, but that was also bolder, more pioneering."

On the other hand, Henry II, who both sides agree deserves most of the credit or blame for firing Hoffman, denies that it was a question of differences relating to either politics ("I don't consider myself a conservative; maybe I am, but I don't think I am") or program ("I'm not at all critical of his program in general; we're still doing most of the same things"). He contends that it was all a matter of management: "I couldn't see how the Foundation could go on the way Paul was running it without falling apart at the seams. I first got an idea of what was happening when Paul took four months off in the spring of 1952 to campaign for Eisenhower's nomination. We didn't object to that, by the way. We gave him the leave of absence, and anyway I was for Eisenhower myself. But during those months I took over some of the administration for the first time—spent one week every month in Pasadena. I found there was no coördination—no contact, even—among the four associate directors. Each one was running his own show, all by himself. There was no teamwork. I tried to build a cohesive, functioning team, as I had at Ford, but I didn't get very far. Later, I met some of the trustees at Hot Springs and told them about conditions in Pasadena. We agreed that the Foundation had to be operated on a businesslike basis."

This is the prevailing view around the Foundation today. "I admire Paul Hoffman," one trustee has observed. "I'm a middle-of-the-road liberal like him. I was all for him to start our new program, and he did a great job, because he's a great visionary. But he couldn't run the thing. If we had had the United States Treasury to draw on and the authority of the United States government to back us up, we couldn't have kept up with Hoffman's ideas. They expanded daily." It is also contended by the present ins that however talented an administrator Hoffman may have been, he just didn't spend enough time on the job; he was constantly leaving Pasadena, they say, to make speeches, attend conferences, receive awards (he is perhaps the most bemedalled and bescrolled citizen in the country), and engage in other activities that had no connection with the foundation he was being paid a reported $75,000 to $100,000 a year to run. His theory was that he was the front man and the director of high policy, and that the associate directors were there to conduct the actual operations. But these were "men of large reputation," strongminded prima donnas, except for Gaither, who was then only on a part-time basis. They either functioned in splendid isolation or, when they did cross one another's path, were as likely to clash as to coöperate. The polar opposites were Katz, whose inductive, or let's-get-the-facts, method was in frequent conflict with Hutchins' deductive, or back-to-first-principles, approach. "It's Francis Bacon Katz versus Thomas Aquinas Hutchins," a member of the staff once remarked.

Experts on foundation work attribute to the Hoffman regime a long list of professional sins: Lines of authority were not clear, as in the case of the two educational Funds set up by Hutchins, which were formally independent but actually dependent on huge annual grants that the trustees of the Foundation in theory could withhold but in practice would have found it extremely embarrassing to; applicants for grants were often turned down brusquely and after long delays, in violation of a basic principle of foundation practice, which is to avert the ire of the rejected grantee by every means short of actually giving him the money; big projects were launched prematurely and with such a fanfare of publicity as to arouse baseless hopes or needless fears; staff executives made public statements without clearing them with the president, who is said to have told one who did bring the draft of a proposed speech to him, "I don't want to see it. Say what you believe— we're for free speech, aren't we?" The president himself was casual about what he said in public. He once delivered a ghost-written speech stating that the Foundation's policy was to spend at least twenty-five per cent of its income overseas; the figure was a dummy one stuck in by the author on the assumption that someone would check it, and no one was more surprised than he when the president publicly committed the Foundation to it. In short, the Hoffman regime's style was dashing rather than canny.

Another difficulty was named Robert Maynard Hutchins. The modern foundation official should be prudent, judicious, diplomatic, and self-effacing, in all of which qualities Hutchins is singularly lacking. Tall, dark, and almost alarmingly handsome, he is as dramatic in behavior as in appearance. Not only is he a "controversial" figure of maximum visibility but he also rather obviously enjoys being one. He likes to tread on dignified toes, he rarely produces the soft answer that turneth away wrath, and his formula for troubled waters does not include oil. He was openly skeptical about the Second World War and given to making pacifist speeches (although some of the early work on the atomic bomb was done under the stands at Stagg Field, where the University of Chicago's football team used to perform until Hutchins abolished it). Many of Hutchins' fellow-educators were shocked by his unorthodox ideas and irritated by statements like "All we can say of American education is that it's a colossal housing project designed to keep young people out of worse places until they can go to work." Clearly, Hutchins was not the foundation type at all, and it is a tribute to Hoffman's salesmanship and to the broadmindedness—and perhaps also to the innocence—of Henry II and his trustees that such a maverick got into the fold even for a while. Once he was in, it was soon manifest that of the four associate directors Hutchins was the one who had both the most "controversial" and the most grandiose ideas about how to spend the Ford millions. Whatever else his educational projects were, they were indisputably big, and this for a while was in his favor, since the Foundation needed to disburse large sums quickly; the trustees were awed by this big-time spender with a big-time vocabulary. But awe is not affection, and as time went on, the trustees felt increasingly resentful at having an arrogant highbrow, who made it plain that he found their logic defective by Aristotelian standards, extract from them each year for his educational Funds over half the money at their disposal. "We felt that that was too big a proportion to be spent on a very special kind of education and that we were in danger of having the bulk of our income committed in advance," Henry II recalls. "I guess we gave it to him because he was the fastest talker. But I didn't like the idea of being a rubber stamp for his ideas." Or, as a non-Ford philanthropoid has put it, "I think Henry was appalled at the speed with which the Foundation was sliding out from under him. He was willing to retire to the sidelines after it had got well launched, as Carnegie and Rockefeller had done, but he wasn't prepared to become emeritus in two years."

Henry II was not the only trustee who began to feel a bit emeritus around the Foundation while Hoffman and Hutchins were running it. The board at the time consisted of Henry and Benson Ford; Frank W. Abrams; John Cowles; Donald K. David; James B. Webber, Jr., a Detroit businessman and an old friend of the Fords (he is the only one who is not still on the board); Charles E. Wilson; and Judge Charles E. Wyzanski, Jr. These were "men of large reputation," too, and the majority agreed with Henry II that it would be well to get in a more amenable set of executives. It was the most drastic purge in the history of the great foundations. The only comparable episode was when Jerome D. Greene resigned in 1917 as executive head of the Rockefeller Foundation. The Rockefeller trustees, frightened by Congressional charges that their foundation was a scheme to spread reactionary ideas, had insisted on restricting future operations to the politically safe fields of medicine and physical science. Although Greene was not fired like Hoffman and made an amicable exit, the facts are that he had been pressing for social science research and that he was replaced by an adept in public relations, George E. Vincent, then president of the University of Minnesota. The Greene resignation, since it was a friendly affair (he later returned to the foundation's board, a kind of reconciliation it is hard to imagine in the more recent instance), did not upset the whole top echelon of executives. The Hoffman purge was all the more remarkable because, since the twenties, foundation staffs have steadily grown more powerful and foundation trustees less. It was as if a late Merovingian king had fired his Mayor of the Palace.

CHAPTER 7

THE NEW ORDER

ON FEBRUARY 5, 1953, the day after Hoffman resigned, Henry Ford II announced that his successor would
be Associate Director Gaither, and that the move to New
York "will not be hurried, but will be carried out in a
gradual and orderly manner"—as, in fact, it was, Gaither
being a gradual and orderly man. One standard American
business type, the high-powered salesman, had been replaced by another, the low-keyed administrator. If Hoffman was the glittering ringmaster of a philanthropic circus,
Gaither is the hard-working transmission belt between the
Ford millions and the outside world; if Hoffman was a crusader, Gaither is a catalyst, precipitating activity without
being affected himself; if Hoffman was the enthusiastic
amateur who rushed in where the trustees feared to tread,
Gaither is the cool professional who never rushes anywhere. His approach is discreet; he dislikes making
speeches or public appearances, and rarely makes any; his
name seldom appears in the newspapers, and then only in
connection with the Foundation.

In the last three years, the outlines of the post-Hoffman
Ford Foundation have emerged in a gradual and orderly
way. More than a year passed before Hoffman's men of

large reputation could be replaced with anonymous younger philanthropoids, namely Dyke Brown, Thomas H. Carroll, William McPeak, and Don K. Price, Jr., all of whom had worked with Gaither on the 1949 Study Report. Two of Hoffman's associate directors, Davis and Katz, resigned with reasonable promptness. "It was fun while it lasted," Davis told the press philosophically; he had almost reached the retiring age, and he had his banking to go back to. Katz returned to the Harvard Law School, where he is now Henry L. Stimson Professor of Law, in an equable state of mind; he is still friendly with the Foundation and draws an annual fee from it as a "program counsellor." The difficulty, once more, was the erinaceous Robert M. Hutchins, who, having resigned as Chancellor of the University of Chicago to become an associate director of the Ford Foundation at a reported $35,000 a year, did not propose to resign again until he had found another position of comparable prestige and salary. Month after month, he rusticated in solitary grandeur in Pasadena, whence all but he had fled, wisecracking to his occasional visitors, "I'm an associate director who doesn't direct anything and doesn't associate with anybody." The dilemma, trying to both parties, was finally resolved in the spring of 1954, when the Fund for the Republic, which he had persuaded the trustees of the Ford Foundation to set up in 1952, and of which the friendly and admiring Hoffman was chairman, made Hutchins its president, at about the same salary he had been getting from the Foundation. The trustees of the Foundation viewed this solution with mixed feelings; Hutchins was off their hands at last, but they could have wished that his troublesome talents had been removed to a greater distance. For although the Fund is wholly independent, and will get no further subsidies from the Foundation in any conceivable future, the press and the public continue to regard it as a branch of the Foundation, and sometimes even confuse the two. (The New

York *Times* described Hutchins as "Associate Director of the Ford Foundation" a whole year after his resignation.)

And, indeed, the Hoffman-Hutchins shadow hung over the Foundation long after the counter-revolution of February 4, 1953. It takes time for a large institution to live down its wild oats, especially when the new administration, for reasons of policy, does not want to admit any sharp break with the old. (Public relations is a two-edged sword.) In the course of his appeal to Congress in the summer of 1953 for a second investigation of foundations, Congressman B. Carroll Reece insisted that Hutchins was still the guiding spirit of the Ford Foundation. "His formal position is that of associate director but, in effect, he has been running the Foundation," Reece said. "Gaither is a mere figurehead [who] . . . has accepted the presidency only for a year, and thus Hutchins may yet become the formal head of the organization." (There was about as much chance of Hutchins becoming head of the Ford Foundation in 1953 as there was of Reece himself getting the job.) At about the same time, Hearst's *Herald & Examiner*, in Los Angeles, took a similar line when it printed an editorial calling on the board of education to turn down a grant of $335,000 from the Fund for the Advancement of Education. The grant was for the purpose of training more teachers for the understaffed local high schools, and the paper reasoned that since Hoffman was a supporter of UNESCO, its real aim was to inoculate the pupils with globalist ideas. "Hoffman is out of the Ford Foundation, but his spirit is still there," the editorial wound up. Duly alarmed, the board of education voted to rescind their acceptance of the tainted $335,000.

The front page of the *Times* of October 27, 1955, carried two stories that illustrate the Foundation's continuing difficulties. One was a report on the first examination for the National Merit Scholarships, on which the Foundation is spending $20,000,000; some 60,000 high-school students throughout the country took the examination, and each of the top four hundred (more or less) will be given a scholarship for four years of college, the precise amount in each case depending on the individual's need. This is plainly commendable; even the Honorable Brazilla Carroll Reece has found nothing to criticize. But the other item reported the resignation from the board of the Fund for the Republic of Arthur H. Dean, who was the American peace negotiator in Korea and is a senior partner of the law firm of Sullivan & Cromwell. Although Mr. Dean was unwilling to specify the "policy reasons" that led him to resign, one story is that he was disgruntled when Hutchins told his board he had hired, as temporary press officer, a former Communist who had a short time earlier "taken the Fifth" and refused to tell a Congressional committee whether he had been a Party member or not; what stuck in Mr. Dean's craw is said to have been not so much the hiring as the fact that the high-riding Hutchins told the board about it *after* he had done it. Another speculation is that Mr. Dean was reacting to the recent drumfire of attacks on what the *Times* delicately called "the often controversial fund"—especially that of National Commander Collins, who urged the American Legion convention last September to boycott the Fund on the ground that it is "threatening . . . the national security." In any case, the good effects of the $20,000,000 in scholarships were offset by the bad publicity given the Foundation's by-blow, Dr. Hutchins' Fund. Yea, verily, the sins of the children shall be visited on the fathers.

In 1949, an important philanthropoid, the late Edwin R. Embree, published an article in *Harper's* entitled "Timid Billions." It caused a sensation in philanthropoidal circles and appears to have influenced the thinking of the Gaither committee that was then writing the Study Report.

Medicine and health meant pioneering fifty years ago; today they are the philanthropic fashion, so firmly established that governments and private individuals support them abundantly [Embree wrote]. Yet the best reports available show that almost half of all foundation appropriations still go to these fields. Another third goes to colleges and universities and various phases of education. Support of welfare agencies and research in the natural sciences account for much of the rest of foundation giving.

Even in these conventional fields, foundations are tending more and more to avoid enterprise and initiative. Instead of pouring brains and money into frontal attacks on fresh problems, they now tend toward what Frederick Gates used to call the great foundation sin, "scatteration"—that is, the sprinkling of little grants over a multiplicity of causes and institutions.

The Ford Foundation's Study Report recommended no spending on medicine, health, welfare agencies, or the natural (that is, physical) sciences. It also echoed Embree's caution against "scatteration," although for a foundation as huge as Ford the warning seemed to be superfluous until recently, since the size of its income makes big programs a technical necessity. Embree also criticized foundations in which the founder's family dominated the board, especially if there was a business angle, and he had some harsh words to say about the then widespread refusal of foundations to give out information about themselves. (On the latter point, he noted that in making a survey he had been unable to get any information at all from 240 out of 505 large foundations canvassed, and that while "the Ford Foundation is reputed to have assets even greater than the Rockefeller or Carnegie endowments . . . this Foundation during all the years of its existence has never made any report to the public.") These complaints, too, were taken to heart at Ford. The Foundation's board was purged of family friends, and its policy on giving out information speedily progressed from reluctance to willingness to eagerness; in fact, some critics now think that it is entirely too public-relations conscious, and accuse it of grabbing headlines. Finally, Embree outlined the fresh fields and pastures new in which the large foundations of today "can turn their energies to social pioneering as heroic as any of the achievements of the earlier days." These fields were teacher education ("America has developed good professional training in medicine, law, and engineering. We have sadly neglected preparation for the most important profession, teaching. The need is not for more or bigger normal schools and teachers' colleges. God forbid!" Hutchins' Fund for the Advancement of Education was the Ford response); "heroic development of the human studies" (the Foundation reacted by setting up its Behavioral Sciences Program); human relations (which Embree defined mainly as fighting against social and political discrimination, and which Ford did something about by establishing its Fund for the Republic); the arts (nothing doing); a great university for the South (ditto); and "world peace and prosperity" (the Foundation plunged in with both feet).

The Foundation is now backing away from Embree's heterodoxy. The $290,000,000 it is going to spend in the next eighteen months for hospitals and medical schools comes under "medicine and health," which Embree saw as the chief "conventional field" of foundation activity, while the $210,000,000 to raise faculty salaries comes as clearly under his second most popular conventional field. The only one of Embree's proposed new fields that the Foundation still cultivates as intensively as ever is "heroic development of the human studies"—and there are those who question, if not the heroism, at least the sagacity of its Behavioral Sciences Program. While the Foundation continues to be greatly concerned with Embree's "world peace and prosperity" (as is indicated by its appointment last fall of a new vice-president for overseas development), its spending on its international program has nevertheless dropped from thirty-five per cent of its total budget under Hoffman to twenty-seven per cent in 1954. Moreover, it has washed its hands of the Fund for the Republic, and by far the largest part of its educational spending now by-passes the experimentally inclined Fund for the Advancement of Education. It is also planning to enter the "conventional field" of physical science. In short, the Bold New Look under Hoffman has given way to Safety First under Gaither. For instance, practically all of the $14,-000,000 spent since 1950 in the eminently safe and sane Area III—The Strengthening of the Economy—has been appropriated under Gaither, a third of it within the past year. Many of the 1955 grants show which way the wind is blowing, such as $150,000 to the American Heritage Foundation for "a national, nonpartisan register-and-vote campaign," and $250,000 to the American Council to Improve Our Neighborhoods, and $600,000 to the National Probation and Parole Association for a five-year study of juvenile delinquency that is described as an "analysis of the possibilities for constructive action." (A foundation never attacks a problem, it sneaks up on it.) Last fall, furthermore, Donald David, shortly after his resignation as Dean of the Harvard Business School, became chairman of the executive committee of the Foundation's board of trustees; he has taken over an office in the Foundation's headquarters, where, for two or three days each week, he works with the officers and deals with matters of general policy. A trustee-in-residence, so to speak, is an innovation in foundation procedure that emphasizes more strongly than ever the greater role of the Ford trustees since Gaither became president. Some observers, in the light of the Foundation's growing conservatism, see a particular significance in the choice of Mr. David, a conservative-minded man who represents the Foundation on the board of the Ford Motor Company and who has always been very close to Henry II.

On the other hand, there is talk around the Foundation which suggests that it may, at some time in the visible future, enter an area that it ignored under Hoffman and that is perhaps the one most neglected by our great foundations—the arts and humanities. "It is amazing that American foundations have done so little for the arts," Embree wrote. "The great emphasis of American philanthropy has been on scholarship and social reform." Abraham Flexner, in *Funds and Foundations*, puts it even more strongly. "America has been oversold on science," he quotes a scientist as saying, and elsewhere states: "No scientist, no psychiatrist, no psychoanalyst, no behaviorist had to teach the authors of oriental texts and the Bible, Shakespeare, Molière, Dante, and Goethe the proper relations between human beings. . . . Justices Holmes and Brandeis are credited with having broadened the field of judicial decision by interpreting legislation in the light of historic and social conditions, but one asks oneself whence did these great judges derive their . . . enlightened point of view? Were they in their growing years given to reading the multitudinous studies in social science, so-called, patronized by the great foundations?"

In another part of his book, Mr. Flexner asks a couple of searching rhetorical questions: "The sciences, medicine, and engineering have their palaces not only in schools of technology but in universities; but where is the university that possesses a palace (or even decent, attractive, and well-equipped halls, libraries, or lecture rooms) for English literature, history, classical studies, and art? . . . No foundation has interested itself in this—one might fairly say—most crying need of modern America. Can one imagine the triumphant shout of approval that would greet such action?"

It remains to be seen whether such a triumphant shout will arise because of anything the Ford Foundation does. Its philanthropoidal style has always been scientific rather than cultural, utilitarian rather than aesthetic. In this, it is more quintessentially American than the Carnegie and Rockefeller foundations, which do have programs in the humanities, however modest and feeble. As President Gaither told the Reece Committee, "The Foundation shares the faith of this country in scientific knowledge and education." The Ford Foundation's two major ventures in the arts to date—the literary magazine *Perspectives USA* and the TV show "Omnibus"—give little reason for optimism about its ability to nourish the Promethean fires. But predictions in this field are risky, since the element of personal taste and imagination is the decisive one, and if the Foundation, by luck or good management, finds a twentieth-century Lorenzo de' Medici, or even a modern Dr. Johnson, to direct its arts-and-humanities division—which will probably be called, when, as, and if it materializes, "Area VI. Democratic Progress in Culture"—the skeptics may be confounded. Or, again, they may not.

There is at least one way, though, in which the Foundation has not changed radically, and that is in its willingness to take on some very large orders, intellectually speaking. As a philanthropoidal philosopher, the Ford Foundation is *sui generis*. Fordian intellection reached its greatest scope, as might be expected, in the era of Hoffman and Hutchins. In addition to the money invested in projects to produce a plan for universal disarmament and to discover "the conditions of peace," it paid $50,000 to the Advertising Council for "a restatement of the principles of American society," out of which came a picture book; $171,000 to the late Russell Davenport's magnificently named Institute for Creative Research for "a study of the fundamentals, workings, and problems of democratic society," out of which came an exposition (unfavorable) on elementary Marxism and another (favorable) on advanced anthroposophy; and $50,000 to the American Committee on United Europe for "research on a European constitution," out of which came research but no constitution. The farthest north was reached, of course, by Dr. Mortimer Adler's Institute for Philosophical Research. Dr. Adler was also a key figure in a project that, had it materialized, would have taken the Foundation all the way to the North Pole and a bit beyond—an Academy of Universal Knowledge, as it were, staffed with distinguished Thinkers who were to devote their collective brains to solving the problems of the world. This, however, proved too grandiose even for the Foundation's Cecil B. deMille imagination, and it was finally abandoned.

Although the new, or Gaitherized, Foundation doesn't go in for dialectical examinations of Western thought or quests for the conditions of peace, it, too, has a weakness for cerebration.

Last year, it divided the considerable sum of $6,500,000 among six law schools to enable them to "develop a program of international studies." The logic behind this project is as impeccable as it is far-fetched. Assumption A is that it is desirable for Americans to become more internationally minded. Assumption B is that, of all kinds of Americans, lawyers are the most important as leaders of public opinion. (Two out of three congressmen are lawyers.) Therefore, the Foundation is spending $6,500,000, with perhaps $10,000,000 to be added as other law schools come into the program, on making law students more internationally minded, whatever that means.

Along the same high-stepping lines, there is a "study of intercultural relations," directed by Professor Robert Redfield, of the University of Chicago, which was begun under Hoffman but has been enthusiastically continued under Gaither. It has already cost $275,000 and is expected to cost $100,000 more by 1957, with the end not yet in sight. Its aim is "to coördinate and improve methods for the comparative study of the major contemporary civilizations of Asia and of their interactions with the West." One thing

Professor Redfield hopes to accomplish is an "improvement of understanding of the persisting and influential characteristics of the principal cultures of mankind." Another is to further "the movement toward common understanding . . . at the level of systematic thought brought into relation with the special knowledge of the scientist and scholar." A third is world peace, just like that. The budget reads like an academic W.P.A. One scholar got $15,000 to finance his "researches in Western civilization," another got $12,361.23 for "a study of the universal modes of apprehension of reality," and a third got $170 for "contributing a study of Islamic susceptibility to Marxism"; two Conferences on Chinese Thought ran up tabs of over $5,000 each, a seminar on Indian village life cost $2,053, and a Conference on Ethnolinguistics cost $4,654. It is unlikely that nothing of significance has come out of all this—how much depends on the quality of the individual scholars concerned—but it is also unlikely that the show will ever live up to Professor Redfield's advance billing.

The shape of the post-Hoffman Ford Foundation is beginning to jell. It has by no means hardened yet, but the main outlines are set. Everything is now centralized at 477 Madison Avenue (at one point the Foundation had eighteen different leases, scattered from Pasadena to New York), and the members of Gaither's new executive team seem to be working in amity among themselves and with the trustees. "The Foundation was more daring and imaginative, also sometimes more foolish, under Hoffman and Hutchins," one scholar who has received grants from both regimes observed a while ago. "They'd grab a bright idea right away, just on the say-so of somebody they trusted. But now it has to go through all sorts of committees. They don't make the mistakes they used to, but they don't take the chances, either. It's become a well-oiled operation, smoothly conveying the dough from the trustees to the grantees." At the quarterly meeting in March, 1955, the trustees approved three big programs, on which they expect to spend $85,000,000—almost all of it in the next three years. At its present rate of spending, these three programs alone would account for nearly half the Foundation's regular annual budget through 1957. But the nature rather than the size of the three programs was what was really significant. In addition to the $20,000,000 National Merit Scholarships, there was a $50,000,000 program to raise the salaries of college teachers and a $15,000,000 fund for research, during the next five to ten years, into the cause and cure of mental illnesss. These are good and necessary enterprises. Many bright students will always need to be helped through college (Dr. Charles C. Cole, Jr., Assistant Dean of Columbia College, recently put the number of talented high-school students unable to go to college for lack of money at 100,000); professors' salaries are notoriously low (a 1953 survey found a range of from $3,200 for instructors to $7,300 for full professors, and stated that to restore academic salaries to their 1940 purchasing power would require at least a twenty-per-cent increase); and mental-health research is amazingly neglected, considering how neurosis-conscious we have become (the national total spent on it at present is only about $7,000,000 a year, almost all of it government money). They are good works, but good works that will in no wise disturb the status quo. They are about as daring as the March of Dimes or the Community Chest. Their attractiveness for Gaither and his associates was precisely that they offered the maximum possibilities for spending money and the minimum danger of getting into "controversial" territory.

But even this program was not large enough, and not safe enough, for the well-Gaitherized Foundation, and at the end of 1955 another was announced that was even safer and a great deal bigger. With the usual opening fanfare of foundationese, like the blaring marches with which a newsreel begins, the Foundation announced last December: "To supplement and encourage the efforts of the American people in meeting problems affecting the progress of the whole nation, the trustees of the Ford Foundation have approved special appropriations of $500,000,000 for privately supported institutions in communities all over the land." It took the Rockefeller Foundation forty years to give away the sum which the Ford Foundation now proposed to divide in the next eighteen months between the nation's colleges, hospitals, and medical schools. (The $50,-000,000 appropriated for college salary increases in March, 1955, will be given out as a bonus to those colleges which the Foundation feels have done the best job of raising teachers' salaries. Unto them that hath shall be given.)

For once, the Foundation seemed to have done something that everybody—everybody whose opinion gets into the papers, that is—agreed was Constructive, Sound, and Forward-Looking. The President of Harvard said that the gift for professors' salaries was timely and seriously needed, diplomatically adding: "The gifts to hospitals and medical schools are no less timely nor any less seriously needed." The President of Yale said it was "a magnificent trailblazing action giving new strength to American education." The President of the American Medical Association said it was "inspiring and heartening to all those who are dedicated to alleviating human suffering." The Chancellor of New York University said that "these magnificent grants will greatly strengthen education in America," and the New York *Herald-Tribune* printed an editorial whose thought—running along a course as familiar as, though a good deal more predictable than, that of a ball in a pinball machine—after ricocheting off "an awesome sum" (flash!), "this magnificent act of philanthropy" (flash!), "strikes at a basic problem" (flash!), and "these epic bequests" (flash! and also *sic*), finally dropped into the pay-off slot: "To channelize $500,000,000 into America's well-being is a tre-

mendous responsibility. It is hard to see how the Ford
Foundation trustees could have better discharged it. They
have won the gratitude of the nation." (Bells ring, colored
lights go on and off, and a spirited rendition is given of
"The Stars and Stripes Forever.") One Marion B. Folsom
predicted that the Ford grants will "contribute signifi-
cantly to the well-being of the American people" because
they "typify the American spirit—the spirit of constructive
philanthropy by private enterprise in the best interests of
the nation." This is just the way a Secretary of Health,
Education and Welfare ought to talk, and Mr. Folsom,
happily, occupies precisely that post in Eisenhower's
cabinet.

The most bitter, implacable, and inveterate of the Foundation's critics were either respectful or silent: "GIFT FOR
GOOD," the New York Hearst paper, the *Journal-American*,
headlined its editorial; "FINE WORK, MR. FORD!" the breezier
but equally illiberal New York *Daily News* put over its
editorial tribute; the cat seemed to have gotten the tongues
of Westbrook Pegler and George Sokolsky, and even the
untiring, unhasting, unresting Fulton Lewis, Jr., although
he continued into its fifth month his radio marathon on
the misuse of Henry Ford's billions, had to admit that this
particular half-billion appeared to be dedicated to non-
subversive purposes—"on the face of it," anyway. About
the only critical view expressed publicly was that of Raymond Dooley, president of a junior college in Lincoln,
Illinois, who wrote the Foundation an open letter point-
ing out the one obvious defect in its program—its failure to
include junior colleges.

There was one aspect of the great give-away which
might have been criticized, but which was not, at least in
public; namely, its lack of imagination. Philanthropoids
commonly speak of the money they handle as "venture
capital," which they invest on the Frontiers of Social
Change or in Long-Range Experiment, taking risks of un-

popularity and of failure which government money cannot take. (This is, indeed one of the principal justifications they give for foundation money being exempt from taxes.) "As old problems come nearer to solution and new problems arise," President Gaither wrote the Reece Committee in 1954, "the Foundation must be able to respond and to move in new directions. We will make mistakes and may incur criticism. But our usefulness is really at an end if we become more interested in playing it safe than in serving humanity." It is only charitable to conclude that he was carried away by foundationese, for the half-billion his Foundation gave away a year or so later dealt with no new problems, moved in no new directions, and generally played it safe. Another victim of this insidious language was Devereux Josephs, chairman of the New York Life Insurance Company. In the state of glassy-eyed euphoria induced by addiction to foundationese, Mr. Josephs, who headed a special committee advising the Foundation on the $210,000,000 college program, recently told a reporter from *The Wall Street Journal:* "You [i.e. the philanthropoids] can easily be too cautious as well as too adventuresome. A foundation has to operate at the edge of social change; that's the main thing we have to bear in mind."

But the half-billion program, in which the adventuresome Mr. Josephs played a leading role, operates not at the edge of social change but in the very center of the status quo. The uses to which the money will be put are clearly meritorious—who could object to helping colleges and hospitals?—but it is equally clear that they will only lubricate the machinery, not improve it. As with the handing out of turkeys to the poor on Thanksgiving, no humane person could object and no imaginative one could applaud. And even granting, just for the sake of argument, that the medical and educational systems as a whole are so close to perfection that they cannot be radically altered without more loss than gain, still it is, as the lawyers say, a matter of common

knowledge that within any given general system some specific institutions perform better than others do. The Foundation, however, ventured no qualitative discrimination:
The amount each institution got was determined entirely
by its size. By the middle of 1957, each of the country's
615 privately supported liberal-arts colleges will have received a sum equal to its 1954–5 faculty payroll. (Even
this criterion has raised an unexpected problem—a number
of colleges are finding that they had a larger payroll for
that year than they had realized before they learned that
the size of their check depended on it.) Each of the country's 3,500 nonprofit private hospitals will get a sum determined by the number of births and patient-days it recorded
in 1954. The whole thing was less a foundation project
than an I.B.M. operation, in which the crucial decisions were
made not by philanthropoids but automatically by the
computing machines into which were fed the raw data and
out of which rolled $99,000 for St. Augustine's College
in Raleigh, North Carolina, $37,300 to Bethany Deaconess
Hospital in Brooklyn, $711,500 to Loyola University in
Chicago, $170,300 to Otterbein College in Westerville,
Ohio, $91,400 to Columbus Hospital in Great Falls, Mon-
tana, $103,400 to Goshen College in Goshen, Indiana,
$4,500,000 to Harvard University, and $5,000,000 (the
largest grant) to New York University.

For all its Hollywoodian scale, this is not a program in
the tradition of the golden age, when Carnegie's and
Rockefeller's foundations concentrated their giving in massive enough doses to bring about basic changes. It is, on the
contrary, a classic example of "scatteration" giving to
which all the classic objections apply. It is merely pallia-
tive, making the status quo a little more endurable but not
encouraging basic solutions. It does not discriminate between the good and the mediocre, but, like the rain, falls
on the just and the unjust alike. (N.Y.U. would be included in few lists of the top American universities.) And

because it covers literally everybody, it is more of a drizzle than a good solid farmer's rain. It doesn't precipitate in any one place enough to make things grow. (The teachers in the 615 colleges will get a raise of about four per cent, a kind of tip which will not go far toward solving the budgetary problems of the most underpaid instructor, and which will still leave academic salaries sixteen per cent behind 1940.) If the half-billion had been used as venture capital, to "respond and move in new directions" and to "operate at the edge of social change," the philanthropoids in charge would have used it to further what they thought were desirable reforms (cf. the Fund for the Advancement of Education and its Arkansas Plan) or to strengthen those institutions they thought were doing a specially good job (cf. Flexner's selection of Johns Hopkins as the model for the reconstruction of the medical schools). To have done either, however, they would have had to know what they thought, and to have been willing to stick their necks out in that direction. While one might imagine it part of a philanthropoid's professional qualifications to have this kind of sophistication and this kind of daring, the fact is he, often, doesn't.

In the present instance, the trouble was probably more lack of daring than of sophistication; the philanthropoids at Ford are reasonably intelligent and knowledgeable men, and it is unlikely that it didn't occur to them that a more productive use could have been made of half a billion dollars than just giving it out, pro rata, to everybody. They were scared, or more accurately, Henry Ford II, Donald David, and the other trustees were scared, and the fear communicated itself, through channels, to the philanthropoids who run the Foundation for them. Large foundations, like large corporations, are timid beasts, and when they are frightened by some small but vocal minority they envelop themselves in a cloud of public relations. As we have seen, the Foundation and its offspring have been under

heavy and persistent attack from ultra-nationalist Congress-
men and journalists ever since the Hoffman-Hutchins regime, and these attacks have by no means moderated in
recent months. The Fund for the Republic, of course, is its
Achilles heel; as this goes to press, the House Un-American
Activities Committee is threatening a special investigation.
On December 6 last, Fulton Lewis, Jr., quoted on his radio
program from a letter Henry Ford II had written in reply
to an inquiry from a member of the American Legion:
"Despite the fact that I have no legal right to intervene in
the affairs of the Fund for the Republic, I have exercised
my right as a private citizen to question the manner in
which the Fund has attempted to achieve its stated objectives. Some of its actions, I feel, have been dubious in
character and inevitably have led to charges of poor judg-
ment." The letter was one of what the New York *Times*
called "several hundred basically identical letters" sent out
over Mr. Ford's signature to people who had been stimulated to write him either by Mr. Lewis or by William
Buckley, Jr., in his new *National Review.* Although it
failed to state which of the Fund's actions Mr. Ford, as a
private citizen, felt had been dubious—since it was an exercise in public relations rather than a serious attempt to
illuminate the problem—it probably had some mollifying
effect on the Foundation's critics. The almost simultaneous
half-billion give-away program, whose public relations
effectiveness was not diminished by the extraordinarily
large number of Catholic colleges and hospitals it included,
has undoubtedly been far more successful as a gesture of
appeasement. It may be that the Ford Foundation will no
longer have to fear Westbrook Pegler, George Sokolsky,
Fulton Lewis, Jr., William Buckley, Jr., or even the Hon.
Brazilla Carroll Reece. Fear no more the heat o' the Right,
or the furious crackpots' rages . . . but the original, let us
remember, was written about the dead.

It may also be that it didn't have to fear them very much

in the first place. Ford Motors has kept on making new records in sales and profits through the last five years, in spite of all the unfavorable publicity received by the Foundation; and early in January, a few weeks before the stock sale, the public demand to be permitted to buy some of the Foundation's Ford stock had reached such a hysterical intensity that Mr. Ford felt it necessary to try to dampen the enthusiasm. "I think some people are indulging in wishful thinking about their chances for fast and fabulous financial gains," he told a mass meeting of securities dealers who were going to handle the issue. As for the Foundation itself, the Gallup poll and the nation-wide editorial comment at the time of the Reece Committee, as already noted, both indicated that, among the public at large, the Foundation's critics are greatly outnumbered by its friends. "The Foundation is cutting loose from the Fund for the Republic because it thinks it is such a hot potato," Beardsley Ruml observed to a journalist last summer. "Or they thought it was anyway. But what are they so scared of? Why are they so insecure? Why do they keep telling the world they have no responsibility for the Fund? The Carnegie people took the Hiss affair in their stride. They didn't feel they had to keep explaining that the Carnegie Corporation was different from the Carnegie Endowment for International Peace." But Mr. Ruml, as is well known, is something of a cynic.

The authors of the 1949 Study Report, headed by Gaither and including four of the Foundation's six current vice-presidents, ended up their Magna Carta by proposing that the Foundation should re-appraise its aims and activities every five or ten years in order to take advantage of "the new opportunities created by changed conditions [and] to continue to serve as an influence for a fresh, experimental approach to the improvement of human welfare." Such a reappraisal was evidently made last year, but with results that were the opposite of a "fresh, experimental approach" dedicated to the seizing of "new opportunities."

In announcing its half-billion-dollar program, the Foundation was careful to note: "It will not distort any of the carefully evolved patterns of higher education." This is the new spirit. The old may be represented by the hope that Hutchins expressed in 1951 about the newborn Fund for the Advancement of Education: "It may ultimately result in the reorganization of the educational system."

But that was a long time ago.

APPENDIX: A PRACTICAL
BIBLIOGRAPHY

After the articles which form this book appeared in the *New Yorker*, a number of people called me up or wrote me asking how to go about getting a grant from a foundation. Some of them seemed to think there is some special technique, some Open Sesame to unlock the doors of the treasure cave. If there is, I didn't run across it. Having an entrée through some prominent person or someone favorably known to some top philanthropoid is probably useful in getting in "to see some one" (besides Mr. X), but special influence, as far as I could determine, rarely affects the actual giving or not giving of the grant. Philanthropoids are wary old birds with much experience at resisting pressure—also with certain standards, not always imaginative but always firm, which they seriously try to live up to—and a too enthusiastic use of personal influence may have a kick-back. "That fellow is trying to come in three doors at once," a Ford executive observed disgustedly about one such tactician.

The criteria on which the philanthropoid makes up his mind are, basically, two. One is the nature and the quality of the project. Does it come within the foundation's program? If so, how well worked-out is it and how promising as to results? If it supplements other projects already being subsidized, its chances of acceptance are greater (though they are less if it *duplicates* existing projects; the line is a delicate one). The other criterion, and the more important, is how much confidence the philanthropoid-in-charge feels in the person or the group which is asking for money. Most large foundations make this easier for themselves by only giving grants through colleges or other institutions, it being much easier to evaluate an institution than an individual. Even when a grant is made direct to an individual, as in fellowships, it helps to be connected with a prestige-heavy institution.

Since one cannot do anything about this second criterion, about the only useful thing the would-be grantee can do, besides making sure one has a sound project (or, more accurately, one the philanthropoids-in-charge will think is sound) is to do some homework before applying. One should know something about the way foundations work, the kind of thing they give money to, the differences between them, and which ones are most likely to be interested in a given project.

Surprisingly little has been written about foundations, considering how important they have been in American life for several generations. And a good deal of what has been written is either very specialized and technical or else superficial and sensationalized. The annual reports of the larger foundations—which may usually be had on request—give details on current grants. And a few books and articles are worth reading, either for current information or for general background.

(A) CURRENT INFORMATION

American Foundations Information Service (860 Broadway, New York 3, N.Y.): *American Foundations and their Fields* (7th edition, 1955)

> A huge reference work, costing $35, which lists and describes 3,500 "true foundations" (the 6th edition, in 1948, covered only 464). As unique and authoritative, in its field, as the phone book. The A.F.I.S. also publishes *The American Foundation News Service*, a periodical bulletin about current developments in the foundation field.

Andrews, F. Emerson: *Philanthropic Foundations* (Russell Sage Foundation, 1956, 459 pp.)

> The most up-to-date detailed survey of the various types of foundations now in existence, with special attention given to 77 of the larger ones. Chapters on organization, finances, operating policies, reporting and publicity, etc.; a very useful section on "Applications for Grants"; and a separate chapter reporting a special study of foundation contributions to scientific research and development in the U.S. A bargain at $5.

Business Week (June 19, 1954): "Business and Foundations—a Special Report to Executives"

> A competent, detailed survey, of more general interest than its title suggests.

"Cox Committee": *Tax Exempt Foundations* (Hearings before the Select Committee to Investigate Tax-Exempt Foundations; House of Representatives, 82nd Congress, 2nd Session, on H. Res. 561; Government Printing Office, Washington, D.C., 1953)

> 792 pages of testimony from all the leading figures in the foundation world—five from Ford alone.

Kiger, Joseph C.: *Operating Principles of the Larger Foundations* (Russell Sage Foundation, 1954, 151 pp.)

> A conscientious and intelligent, if somewhat pedestrian, monograph on the functions, policies and problems of foundations today. By the former research director of the Cox Committee. Bibliography, tables, index, etc.

Whyte, William H., Jr.: "What Are the Foundations Up To?" and "Where the Foundations Fall Down" (*Fortune*, October and November, 1955)

> The October article is a once-over-lightly on the "Big Three" (Ford, Rockefeller, Carnegie); it has a special section, "How to Get a Grant," on the right way and the wrong way to set up an academic research project. The November article cuts much deeper; it is a well-documented and closely reasoned indictment of the foundations for neglecting the individual scholar.

(B) GENERAL BACKGROUND

Embree, Edwin R.: "The Business of Giving Money" (*Harper's*, August, 1930); "Timid Billions" (*Harper's*, March, 1949)

> Two important discussions of general policy by one of the leading philanthropoids of the twenties and thirties.

Flexner, Abraham: *Funds and Foundations* (Harper, 1952, 146 pp.)

> Diffuse and rambling, but valuable because of the historical information and the informed and acute criticism of present-day foundation policy which Dr. Flexner is uniquely able to provide out of his long and fruitful career as a philanthropoid.

Ford Foundation: *Report of the Study on Policy and Program* (Ford Foundation, Detroit, Mich., 1949)

> Mostly ancient history now, but the last chapter on "The Administration of the Program," by Don Price, a vice-president

of the Foundation, still gives about the best inside view of
foundation grant-making procedures.

Keppel, Frederick P.: *The Foundation* (Macmillan, 1930, 113 pp.)
This little book, by a celebrated former head of Carnegie Corporation, was originally a series of lectures. Discursive, thoughtful, sophisticated, it is an intelligent introduction to the subject.

Laski, Harold J.: "Foundations, Universities, and Research" (a
chapter in his book, *Dangers of Obedience*; Harper, 1930)
A witty and eloquent summing up of the case against foundations as an influence on scholarship.

Lindeman, Eduard C.: *Wealth and Culture* (Harcourt, 1936)
A muck-raking survey, from a conventional-liberal point of
view, that is now outdated as to many of its specific complaints (as, that philanthropoids are arrogant and secretive) but
which is still to the point in more general criticisms (as, that
business types are over-represented on foundation boards and
intellectuals represented hardly at all).

Tunks, Lehan K.: *The Modern Philanthropic Foundation and
Private Property* (Unpublished thesis, 1947; on deposit at the Yale
Law School)
Contains a great deal of information—legal, economic, and just
plain curious—from which I have drawn considerably for the
historical chapter in this book. Mr. Tunks is now dean of the
Rutgers Law School. The chief topic of his thesis is the re-
lation, in legal terms, of the foundation and property rights.
(On this, also cf. Berrien C. Eaton's articles in the *Virginia
Law Review* of November and December, 1949, and the arti-
cle by the editors of the *Yale Law Journal* in their issue of
February, 1950.)

INDEX

ABC network, 63
Abrams, Charles, 91-3
Abrams, Frank W., 16, 51, 153
Accent, 86
Acheson, Dean, 27
Adler, Dr. Mortimer J., 30, 54-5, 164
Adult Education Assn., 57
Advertising Council, 30, 163
African Abstracts, 64
Agricultural Adjustment Admin., 143
Agriculture, U.S. Dept. of, 13, 48, 98
Air Force, 10
Alabama Prison Board, 114
Alaska Rural Rehabilitation Corp., 98
Alexander the Great, 110
Albert and Mary Lasker Foundation, 39
Albright, Horace M., 85
Allen, Fredrick Lewis, 7
Altschul, Frank, 25
Aluminium, Ltd., 91
Amalfis, 14
American Assn. of Colleges for Teacher Education, 52
American Bar Assn., 27, 70
American Civil Liberties Union, 75
American Committee on United Europe, 163
American Council of Learned Societies, 63
American Council to Improve Our Neighborhoods, 161
American Foundation for Political Education, 57-8

American Foundation Information Service, 176
American Friends Service Committee, 75
American Heritage Foundation, 161
American Legion, 15, 76, 158
American Medical Assn., 167
American Veterans Committee, 78
American Woolen Co., 42
Andrews, F. Emerson, 36, 176
Ankara library school, 65
Antoninus Pius, 37
Aquinas, Thomas, 54
Architectural Forum, 83
Aristides, 127
Aristotle, 110-11
Arkansas Plan, 52, 118, 171
Arnold, Edwin G., 67
Associated Press, 30
Astor, John Jacob, 40
Atlantic Monthly, 7, 86
Audiology Foundation, 38
Aung, U Hpe, 68-9

Babson, Roger W., 38
Bacon, Francis, 120
Baltimore, Lord, 9
Banking, 30
Baruch, Bernard, 108
Bedingfield, Robert E., 136-7
Beecher, Henry Ward, 101
Beethoven, Ludwig van, 89
Behavorial Sciences Program, 80-4, 160
Bernarr MacFadden Foundation, 39
Benny, Jack, 89
Benson, George, 92-3
Bentham, Jeremy, 81, 120

179